PS I LOVE YOU BABY COLLECTION

8970 E. HAMPDEN AVE. DENVER, CO 80231 (303) 740-6206

LYNDA MILLIGAN AND NANCY SMITH

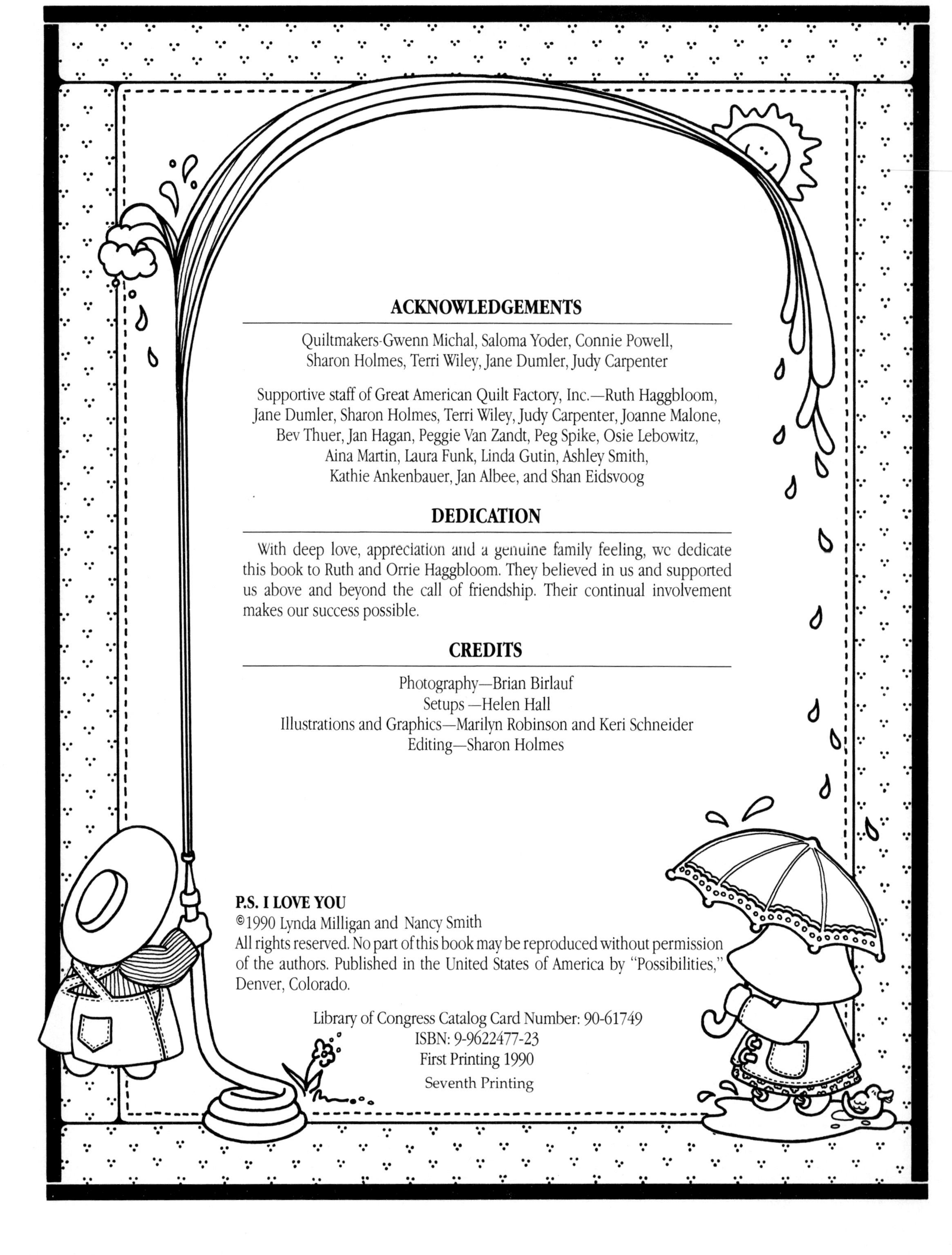

ACKNOWLEDGEMENTS

Quiltmakers-Gwenn Michal, Saloma Yoder, Connie Powell,
Sharon Holmes, Terri Wiley, Jane Dumler, Judy Carpenter

Supportive staff of Great American Quilt Factory, Inc.—Ruth Haggbloom,
Jane Dumler, Sharon Holmes, Terri Wiley, Judy Carpenter, Joanne Malone,
Bev Thuer, Jan Hagan, Peggie Van Zandt, Peg Spike, Osie Lebowitz,
Aina Martin, Laura Funk, Linda Gutin, Ashley Smith,
Kathie Ankenbauer, Jan Albee, and Shan Eidsvoog

DEDICATION

With deep love, appreciation and a genuine family feeling, we dedicate this book to Ruth and Orrie Haggbloom. They believed in us and supported us above and beyond the call of friendship. Their continual involvement makes our success possible.

CREDITS

Photography—Brian Birlauf
Setups —Helen Hall
Illustrations and Graphics—Marilyn Robinson and Keri Schneider
Editing—Sharon Holmes

P.S. I LOVE YOU

 Published in the United States of America by "Possibilities," Denver, Colorado.

Library of Congress Catalog Card Number: 90-61749
ISBN: 9-9622477-23
First Printing 1990
Seventh Printing

TABLE OF CONTENTS

INTRODUCTION

Nothing is more delightful than welcoming a new baby into the world with his or her own quilt—a handmade security blanket. *P.S. I Love You* contains a wealth of projects to inspire the making of distinctive gifts that will become treasured heirlooms.

P.S. I Love You is a comprehensive book that is designed to create an environment that is filled with warmth, love, sharing and caring. The quilts feature easy, intermediate and complex skill levels; homespuns, calicos and bold decorator prints; and hues ranging from soft, muted pastels to bright crayon colors. Each quilt is shown in a room setting that sparks the imagination to make any nursery a one-of-a-kind treasure.

Complete directions, full-size templates and fabric yardage charts for seventeen quilts sized from cradle to twin are included. A complete range of accessories including bumper pads, crib sheets, dust ruffles, a mobile, toys and a doll will help in personalizing a nursery. The *Glossary of Techniques* includes basic information on all phases of hand or machine quiltmaking.

Truly individual gifts will create a bond of love that will warm the hearts of both maker and receiver. *P.S. I Love You* says it all.

TOOLS & SUPPLIES

BACKING—the back or bottom layer of the quilt. It is usually 100% dressweight cotton fabric with a medium thread count. Cotton fabric is much easier to hand quilt and seldom allows batting fiber to "migrate" through the fabric. Sheets generally have too high a thread count, making them extremely difficult to hand quilt. It may be necessary to seam widths of fabric together to accommodate larger quilts. The backing should be 2″ to 3″ larger than the quilt top on each side.

BATTING—a filler used as an interlining between the quilt top and the backing. It provides warmth and thickness. It can be 100% cotton, 100% polyester, or a combination of the two. The higher the cotton content, the more closely the quilt must be quilted. Cotton batting usually has no outside covering on it and thus has a tendency to bunch and shift. Batting is sold in standard bed sizes, from crib size to king size, or may be purchased by the yard. It is available in white or black. Quality batting should be smooth, even, and of uniform thickness.

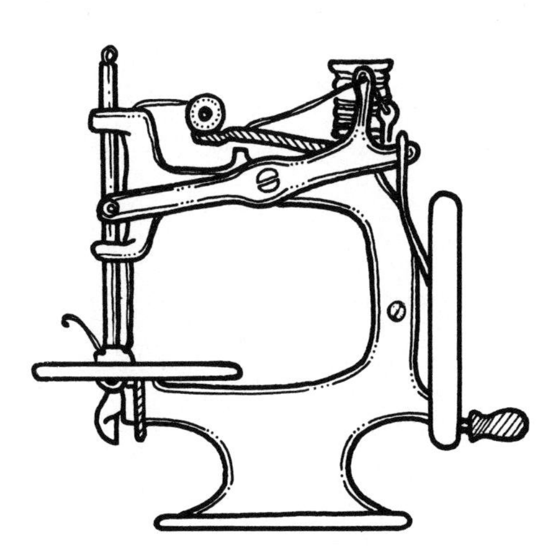

BINDING—the fabric that is used to finish the outer raw edges of the quilt.

BLOCK—a complete pattern or design unit. Often a quilt top is composed of many of the same blocks or variations of those blocks sewn together side by side or separated by sashing strips.

BORDER—a separate outside frame completing or enhancing a central element. It is intended to act as the final statement of a quilt. The border can be made of plain, pieced or appliqued strips. The border can often "make or break" the total effect of a quilt.

CUTTING MAT—a mat made especially for use with the rotary cutter. It has a self-healing surface and comes in various sizes from 4″ square to approximately 23″ × 35″. Mats are available in various colors, and some are printed with a grid. The most usable size for quilting is a mat that measures at least 23″ wide which accommodates a width of folded 45″ fabric.

EVEN-FEED FOOT—an attachment for a sewing machine that keeps the top layer of fabric from being pushed ahead of the bottom layer. It is *very* helpful when machine quilting and when adding binding to a quilt.

FABRIC FOR QUILTMAKING—The recommended fabric for quiltmaking is 100% cotton. Fabric should be of similar dressweight, closely-woven cottons. These natural fibers age at similar rates. Cotton fibers have similar "stretchability" and iron well. Cotton is easy to quilt by hand. Fabrics should be prewashed and checked for colorfastness before using.

FABRIC GLUE—an all-purpose glue that works especially well with fabrics. Aleene's™ "Tacky" glue is one example.

FUSING WEB—a paper-backed bonding agent which is released by ironing. Use it to secure fabric to paper, cardboard, wood, plastic, metal, or another fabric. It is sold by the yard or in prepackaged sizes in craft and fabric stores. Two brand names are Wonder-Under™ and Trans-Web™.

GLUE GUN—an electric gun used to melt sticks of glue which bond surfaces instantly. Guns can be manual or equipped with a finger trigger. Colored glue is also available.

GLUE STICK—solid adhesive in a stick which is easy to use and works well for many craft projects. Keeping the glue stick in the refrigerator will keep it tacky longer.

GRAIN—The *straight* grain can either be lengthwise or crosswise. The lengthwise grain runs parallel to the selvage. This direction has the least amount of stretch. The *crosswise* grain runs at right angles to the selvage and has some stretch. The *bias* is the diagonal of the fabric, the true bias being at a 45° angle to the straight of the grain. It produces maximum stretchability. When sewing with bias and straight grain, put the bias piece underneath, next to the feed dog.

INTERFACING—a stabilizer used in fashion sewing and craft projects. Interfacing can be woven or non-woven, fusible or nonfusible. Most craft projects use non-woven fusible interfacing. Fusible interfacing has stretch in the crosswise direction and is stable in the lengthwise direction. It has no grainline. It is sold for sheer to heavyweight fabrics.

INVISIBLE THREAD—the same as transparent nylon thread or nylon monofilament thread. It is used when an invisible stitch is desired.

IRON—a tool that is essential for quiltmaking and general sewing. It is helpful to have the soleplate of the iron covered with a non-stick finish. The iron should have a large water reservoir for steam, be comfortable to hold, and not be too heavy.

IRONING BOARD—a surface upon which to iron. It is preferable to have a well-cushioned board with an adjustable height. The ironing board cover can be plain or printed with a grid. The gridded cover must be straight if it is being used as a pressing guide.

MIRROR MAGIC © 1990—By using two mirrors set at right angles, it is possible to see what one block reflected into four images looks like. It is equally useful for determining specific miters and multiple star patterns. Directions for a variety of uses are included.

NEEDLEPUNCH/FLEECE—a 100% polyester product used to add dimension to quilted and padded crafts, home decorating projects and garments. It does not stretch like traditional batting and is easy to cut, shape and handle.

NEEDLES—Hand sewing needles are called "sharps," and quilting needles are called "betweens." Both come in sizes from #5 to #12; the higher the number, the finer the needle. Sewing is easier with finer needles, but they are also harder to thread.

ONE-QUARTER INCH MASKING TAPE—a special size of masking tape useful to quilters. Use it to temporarily "mark" for quilting.

PERMANENT MARKING PENS—pens that come in a variety of colors and thicknesses and do not bleed on fabric or fade in the wash. They are excellent to use for signing quilts or quilt labels and for drawing doll faces. The "Pigma" brand is highly recommended. *Always* test ink on a scrap first.

PINEAPPLE RULE—a ruler devised for the construction of pineapple blocks or square-within-a-square patterns. It has horizontal, vertical and radiating 45° markings that help ensure accuracy for template-free cutting and sewing techniques.

QUILT TOP—the front or top layer of the quilt. It can be plain fabric, pieced, appliqued, embroidered, painted, stenciled, or decorated in any way.

QUILTING HOOP—similar to an embroidery hoop but thicker. It is a double wooden circle with a self-contained clamp. The size of the hoop depends on the comfort preference of the individual and the size of the project.

QUILTING STENCILS OR TEMPLATES—used to draw the quilting pattern directly onto the quilt top. Templates or stencils are generally basic outlines or shapes which are filled in with additional detail lines. The shapes can be realistic or geometric and can be used singly or repeated.

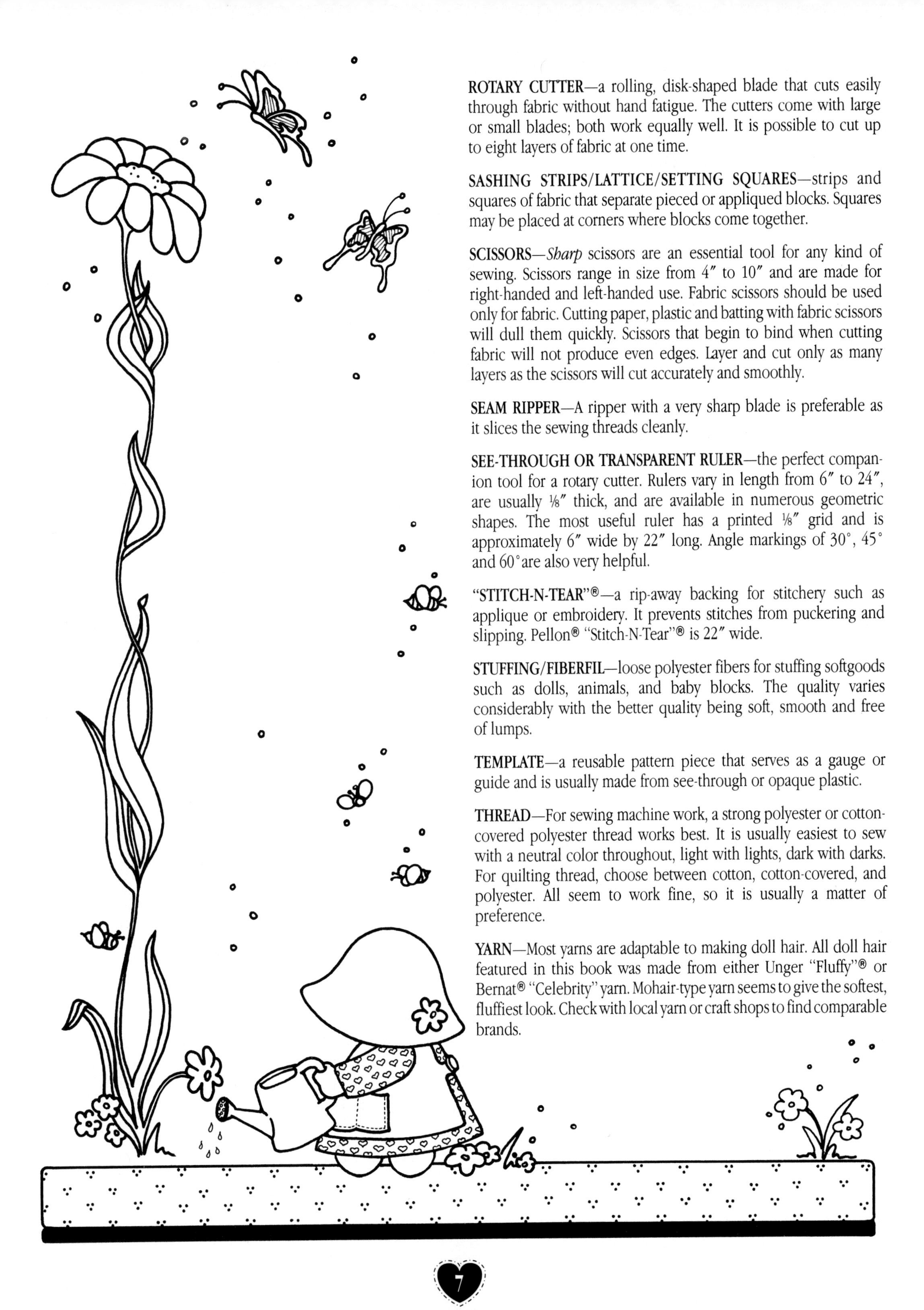

ROTARY CUTTER—a rolling, disk-shaped blade that cuts easily through fabric without hand fatigue. The cutters come with large or small blades; both work equally well. It is possible to cut up to eight layers of fabric at one time.

SASHING STRIPS/LATTICE/SETTING SQUARES—strips and squares of fabric that separate pieced or appliqued blocks. Squares may be placed at corners where blocks come together.

SCISSORS—*Sharp* scissors are an essential tool for any kind of sewing. Scissors range in size from 4″ to 10″ and are made for right-handed and left-handed use. Fabric scissors should be used only for fabric. Cutting paper, plastic and batting with fabric scissors will dull them quickly. Scissors that begin to bind when cutting fabric will not produce even edges. Layer and cut only as many layers as the scissors will cut accurately and smoothly.

SEAM RIPPER—A ripper with a very sharp blade is preferable as it slices the sewing threads cleanly.

SEE-THROUGH OR TRANSPARENT RULER—the perfect companion tool for a rotary cutter. Rulers vary in length from 6″ to 24″, are usually ⅛″ thick, and are available in numerous geometric shapes. The most useful ruler has a printed ⅛″ grid and is approximately 6″ wide by 22″ long. Angle markings of 30°, 45° and 60° are also very helpful.

"STITCH-N-TEAR"®—a rip-away backing for stitchery such as applique or embroidery. It prevents stitches from puckering and slipping. Pellon® "Stitch-N-Tear"® is 22″ wide.

STUFFING/FIBERFIL—loose polyester fibers for stuffing softgoods such as dolls, animals, and baby blocks. The quality varies considerably with the better quality being soft, smooth and free of lumps.

TEMPLATE—a reusable pattern piece that serves as a gauge or guide and is usually made from see-through or opaque plastic.

THREAD—For sewing machine work, a strong polyester or cotton-covered polyester thread works best. It is usually easiest to sew with a neutral color throughout, light with lights, dark with darks. For quilting thread, choose between cotton, cotton-covered, and polyester. All seem to work fine, so it is usually a matter of preference.

YARN—Most yarns are adaptable to making doll hair. All doll hair featured in this book was made from either Unger "Fluffy"® or Bernat® "Celebrity" yarn. Mohair-type yarn seems to give the softest, fluffiest look. Check with local yarn or craft shops to find comparable brands.

GLOSSARY OF TECHNIQUES

FABRIC PREPARATION

Fabrics made of 100% cotton are highly recommended for quilting. All washable fabrics should be laundered before being used in a quilt. Determine if fabrics are colorfast by handwashing separately in detergent and warm water. If the water remains clear, fabrics may be washed together. If any fabric bleeds, wash it separately. If fabric continues to bleed, discard and select another fabric. After checking for colorfastness, wash fabrics in a washing machine with warm water and a mild detergent; rinse well. Tumble dry, as most shrinkage occurs in the dryer. Press, using steam and spray sizing if necessary.

PRESSING

In quilting, seam allowances are pressed to one side or the other. The standard ¼″ seam allowance used in quiltmaking makes it difficult, if not impossible, to press seams open. In addition, the quilt is actually more durable if seams are not pressed open. It is preferable to press seams toward the darker fabric. If this is not possible, make sure dark fabric seams do not show through the quilt top by trimming a scant amount off the dark seam allowance.

1. Press patchwork on the back first, using steam and a gentle, up-and-down motion. Swinging the iron back and forth tends to distort and stretch patchwork. Then turn block or quilt top over and press gently on the right side.
2. When pressing block seams (seams joining one block to another), press all seams in the same direction for one whole row. On the next row, press all block seams in the other direction. This will allow seams to fall in opposite directions when machine sewing one row to another row.
3. When ironing row seams, press the entire seam length of the row in the same direction, always being careful not to stretch the fabric.
4. When ironing border seams, press all seams toward outside edges. A final pressing of the quilt top will make it easier to mark the quilting design and will make potential problem areas visible.

CUTTING FOR MACHINE PIECING

TEMPLATE METHOD

1. Make templates using typing paper or graph paper to include ¼″ seam allowances.
2. Fold or layer fabric (up to eight layers) and press. Hold the paper template in place or tape it to the fabric using a loop of transparent tape. Cut around the template with very sharp scissors, being sure to keep the blades of the scissors at a 90° angle to the fabric so all patches will be the same size. Folding the fabric will automatically produce reverse images of asymmetrical patches. If asymmetrical patches are needed without their reverse images, layer all fabric pieces right side up rather than folding.

3. An alternate method: Fold or layer the fabric as above. Make a plastic template including ¼″ seam allowance. Draw around template with a pencil on top layer of fabric. Pin center of each patch and cut out with sharp scissors.

ROTARY CUTTER METHOD

1. For rotary cutting, begin by laying wrinkle-free, double-folded fabric on a cutting mat. Position it so the single fold and selvage are at the bottom and one raw crossgrain edge is at the right. Using a see-through ruler marked with a right angle, match up the top edge of the ruler (or one of the right-angle lines) with the fold of the fabric. Cut the right edge of the fabric off, resulting in a straight edge from which to begin cutting strips. Swing mat and fabric around 180°. Position the ruler so that the marking for the desired strip width is even with the freshly cut edges of the fabric. Keep the top and bottom edges of fabric parallel to the horizontal lines of the ruler.

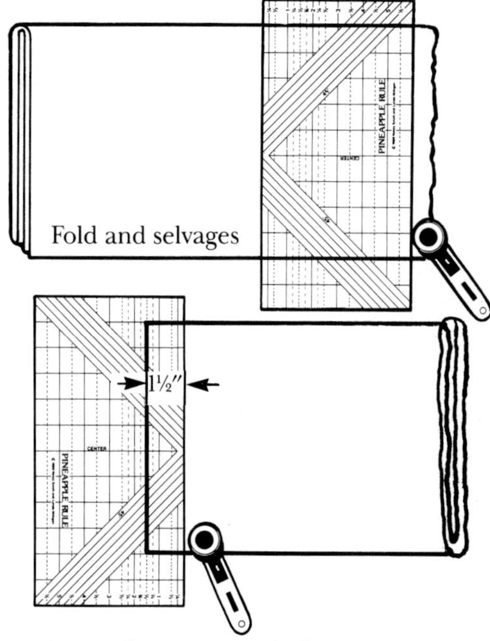

2. Squares can be cut from strips with the rotary cutter. Be sure to include ¼″ seam allowances all around (i.e., for 2″ finished patches, cut the squares 2½″). Layer fabric up to eight layers for maximum speed in cutting.
3. Half-square triangles can be cut from strips with the rotary cutter also, but a formula for the correct added seam allowance must be applied. For example, for half-square triangles to fit next to 2″ finished squares in the same block, 2⅞″ squares are cut first, and then they are cut diagonally into half-square triangles. To figure for any size half-square triangle, simply add ⅞″ to the desired *finished* size using the measurement of the triangle on its short side.
4. Odd-sized and asymmetrical patches can be cut quickly with the rotary cutter by cutting around paper templates. Make sure templates include ¼″ seam allowance. Layer the fabric by folding (reverse image patches will automatically be cut) or stacking fabric pieces with right sides up (all pieces will be exactly the same with no reverse image patches). Tape the pattern to the top layer of fabric with a loop of transparent tape. Using a small rotary cutting ruler (1″ × 12″ or 6″ × 12″), rotary cut around the paper pattern, moving the ruler as needed.

MACHINE PIECING

1. Use a light neutral thread when sewing most fabrics, but if all fabrics are dark, use dark thread. Pattern pieces include seam allowance unless otherwise noted.
2. Using an accurate ¼″ seam allowance, place the pieces to be joined with the right sides together. Pin, matching seamlines, and sew with a straight stitch, 10 to 12 stitches per inch. Press seam allowances to one side, toward the darker fabric, unless otherwise noted.
3. To save time and thread, chain piece by sewing a seam and then immediately feeding in a new set of pieces without lifting presser foot or clipping threads. Sew as many sets as possible in this manner, then clip them apart.
4. Where two seams meet, position one seam allowance in one direction and one seam allowance in the opposing direction. Butt the seams together exactly; they will hold each other in place. It is usually not necessary to pin.
5. When crossing triangular intersection seams, aim for the point where the seamlines intersect. This will avoid cutting off the points in the patchwork design.

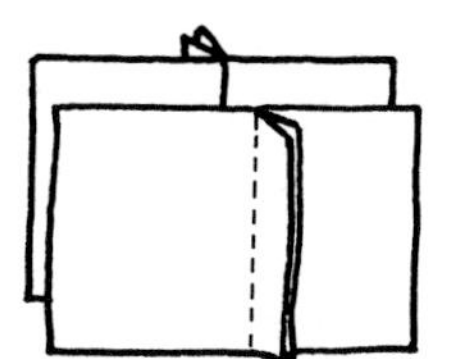
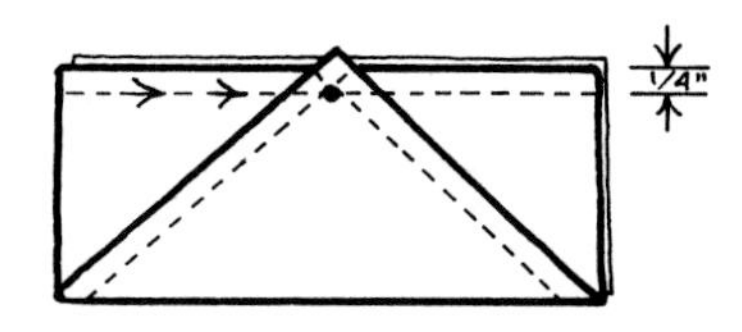

6. If one edge appears to be larger, put that side next to the feed dog of the machine so the extra will be eased into the seam without leaving tucks.
7. To piece the center of a block where eight points come together, begin by sewing four quarter blocks. Press seams as illustrated. Then sew quarters together, making half blocks. Press seam allowances of both halves in the same direction. When halves are placed right sides together, seams will fall in opposite directions. Match halves, butting seams together and aligning intersections. Pin if necessary and stitch.

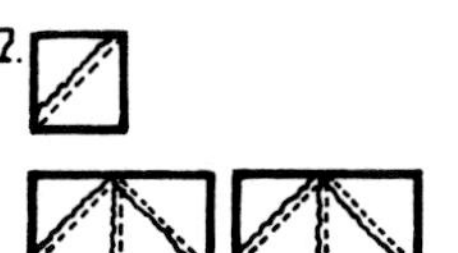

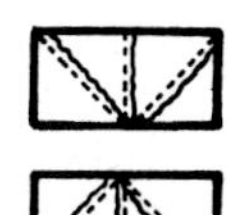
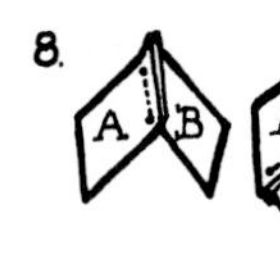

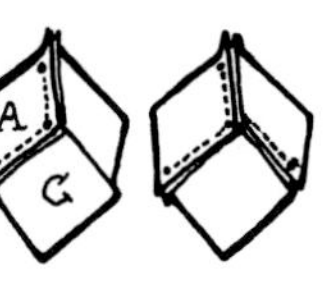

8. To sew set-in pieces: (1) Stitch piece A to piece B, right sides facing and raw edges even. Begin and end stitching ¼″ from edge, backstitching at both beginning and end. (2) Sew C to A, again beginning and ending stitching ¼ ″ from each edge. (3) Sew C to B, also beginning and ending stiching ¼″ from each edge.

HAND PIECING

1. Make templates from patterns. *Do not* include seam allowances.
2. Draw exactly around templates on *wrong* side of fabric. Allow ½″ between templates and at least ¼″ from each edge of fabric. Mark corners clearly and accurately.
3. Cut pieces from fabric, cutting ¼″ *outside* of marked line. Marked line is stitching line.

4. Place pieces right sides together, matching and pinning at corners and intervals along marked lines. All pins should be placed at right angles to the marked sewing line. Remove the corner pin and insert the needle at this point. Take a stitch and then a small backstitch, and then sew with a short, even running stitch, checking from time to time that the marked lines on both front and back match. Remove pins as it becomes necessary. Sew to the end of marked line and backstitch. *Do not sew seam allowances down;* instead slide needle under seam allowances from point to point. This allows seam allowances to be pressed to either side. Assemble into units.

MACHINE APPLIQUE

BONDABLE INTERFACING METHOD

1. Bond medium-weight, iron-on interfacing to back of applique fabric following manufacturer's directions. Cut appliques from bonded fabric. Do not include seam allowance. Use fabric glue stick sparingly to attach appliques to background fabric, layering design from background to foreground.
2. Place a background stabilizer such as typing paper or Pellon® "Stitch N Tear"® under background fabric. Use a very short stitch length and a 1/16" to 1/8" wide zig-zag stitch width. Use a good quality thread. Loosen top tension as needed to keep bobbin thread from being visible on top of work. Keep the threads of the satin stitch at right angles to the edge of the applique by pivoting as needed. To pivot, leave needle in fabric, lift presser foot, turn fabric, lower foot, resume sewing. For outside curves, pivot when needle is on background fabric. For inside curves, pivot when needle is on applique fabric. To make tapered points, reduce stitch width while sewing. To tie off threads, bring stitch width to zero and take 6 to 8 stitches next to the satin stitching. When finished sewing, tear away background stabilizer.

FUSING WEB METHOD (PELLON® "WONDER-UNDER"™ or TRANS-WEB™)

1. Trace patterns onto smooth, paper side of fusing web. *Trace patterns the reverse of the direction wanted.*
2. Press fusing web to wrong side of desired fabric with rough side facing fabric. Cut out shapes.
3. Peel off paper; position applique onto background fabric and press again; applique fuses to background. If design is layered, arrange all appliques before fusing.
4. For sewing, see step 2 under bondable interfacing method above.

HAND APPLIQUE

1. Make templates from patterns without adding seam allowances.
2. Place template down on *right* side of fabric and draw around it.
3. Cut pieces out, cutting 3/16" to 1/4" *outside* of drawn line.
4. Baste under all edges that are not overlapped by another piece by folding edges under on penciled line and basting in place with a single thread.
   a. Clip seam allowance on inside curves, allowing fabric to spread.
   b. Clip inside angles up to seamline. When appliqueing these angles, take small overcast stitches to prevent fraying.
   c. Miter outside points less than 90° in three separate folds: Fold down point; fold one edge to seamline; fold other edge to seamline. It may be necessary to trim corner before folding to reduce bulk.

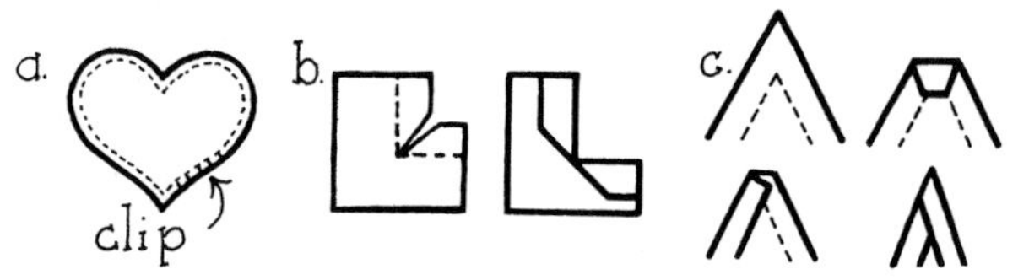

5. Pin or baste pieces to background fabric using pattern as a guide.
6. Using thread to match, applique. Work stitches from right to left. Hide knot under applique or on back. To begin, bring needle up through applique and out the edge of the fold. Directly below where thread emerges from applique, take a tiny stitch through the background fabric, bringing needle point immediately back up into the fold of the applique. Run the needle point along inside the fold for 1/8" to 1/4" and then out through the edge of the fold. Pull thread through. Repeat. Do not press applique pieces.
7. If the work is to be quilted, it is much easier and usually looks nicer if the backing fabric is removed from behind the applique. Working from the wrong side with small, sharp scissors, carefully cut away the backing fabric up to 1/4" from the applique seamline. This also helps avoid the possibility of a darker background fabric showing through a lighter applique shape.

ASSEMBLING

QUILTS SET BLOCK TO BLOCK

1. Begin by laying out all the quilt blocks.Take a few minutes to stand back and view the arrangement. If using sparsely patterned fabric, there may be an area of concentrated color that was not expected. By laying out all blocks, changes can be made before blocks are sewn together. Scrap quilt blocks often need some rearranging. A little bit of red or yellow in one of the fabrics may "pop" out, and distributing this "color" around the quilt may make a much more pleasing arrangement. This is a good time to decide if it would be preferable to separate the blocks with plain or pieced lattice strips and squares.
2. When the arrangement is pleasing, begin assembling. Sew all block units together into rows using a ¼″ seam allowance. Press all seams between block units of odd rows (1, 3, 5, 7, . . .) to the right and all seams between block units of even rows (2, 4, 6, 8, . . .) to the left. When rows are sewn together, seams will butt up against each other and hold each other in place for machine sewing.

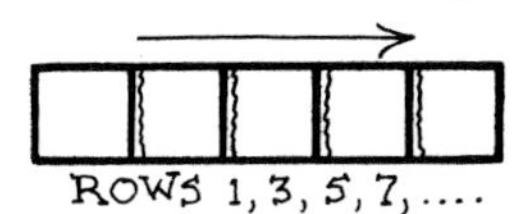

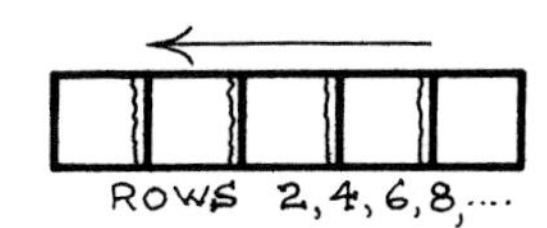

3. Sew row 1 to row 2, row 3 to row 4, row 5 to row 6, and so on. Sew row unit 1-2 to row unit 3-4 and so on. By sewing row *units* together, there will be less bulk than when sewing individual rows together in order. The final row seam will connect the top half of the quilt to the bottom half.

QUILTS SET WITH SASHING

1. Sashing is strips that separate the quilt blocks. Include sashing strips when laying out the quilt to decide on the block arrangement. Sew rows of blocks and vertical sashing strips; press seams toward sashing strips if sashing fabric is darker. Continue sewing blocks to form rows as above.
2. If horizontal sashing strips have no corner setting squares, sew them to block rows. Be careful to align blocks so they match from one row to the next. Press seam allowances toward sashing if sashing fabric is darker.
3. If horizontal sashing strips have corner setting squares, assemble strips and squares for each row. Press the seam allowances *away* from the corner setting squares. These seam allowances will then lay opposite to the seam allowances on the block rows.
4. Row units can be made to reduce bulk as described above in step 2 of assembling quilts set block to block.
5. When all rows are assembled, add side sashing strips and then end sashing strips.

BORDERS

STAIRSTEP BORDERS

Note: Check individual quilt directions for sewing order of quilt borders. All quilt cutting directions give border lengths. Because of differences in fabric stretch and seam allowances, it would be wise to check *your* quilt's measurements.

1. To determine the length of the side borders for any assembled quilt center, measure the length of the quilt from cut edge to cut edge at intervals and take an average of these measurements. Do not use the side edge as one of the measurements.
2. Piece crossgrain cuts of fabric to equal the average length of the quilt center, or cut seamless borders from fabric on the lengthwise grain. Fold the border and the quilt top into quarters and mark with pins. Matching marked points, pin border to quilt, right sides together. If one edge (quilt top or border) is slightly longer, put the longer edge against the feed dog, and the excess fabric will be eased. Take care to see that the pressed seams of the quilt top and border lay flat and do not get twisted.
3. Repeat above process for top and bottom borders.
4. Adding subsequent borders is much easier. The borders previously added can be measured to get the lengths needed for the next ones. Continue adding side borders and then top and bottom borders.
5. Press border seams toward outside edges of quilt unless "show-through" can be prevented by changing pressing directions of border seams.

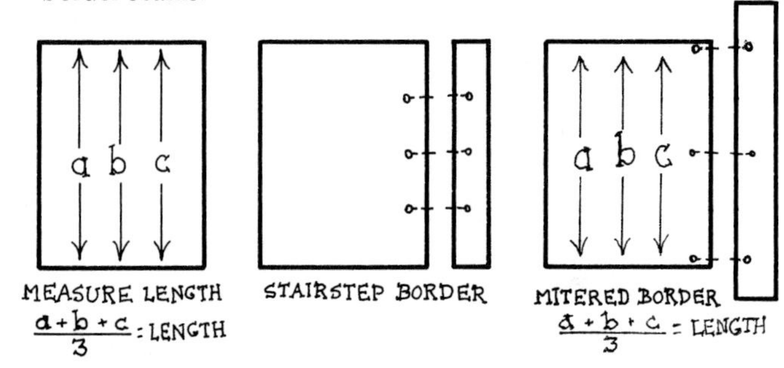

MITERED BORDERS

1. While not difficult, it requires some patience to achieve a terrific mitered corner. To determine the length to prepare the side borders, measure the quilt length without borders as described in step 1 of stairstep borders above. Add to this measurement the width of all planned borders on both ends of the quilt plus 2″ to 4″ for good measure. (The individual quilt cutting measurements in this book already include this extra fabric.) To determine the length to prepare the end borders, measure the quilt width without borders and add the width of all planned borders on both sides of the quilt plus the 2″ to 4″ extra. Stitch crossgrain cuts of fabric together, if necessary, to make the needed lengths, or cut seamless borders on the lengthwise grain. If the quilt has more than one border, sew individual borders for each side together first to make complete border units. More fabric may be needed, but the corners are much easier to miter. Press seam allowances toward what will be the outside edge of the quilt.
2. Measure the length of the quilt without borders *from seamline to seamline* by measuring down the middle of the quilt in several places, *not* at the edge. Find the center of the long, inside edge of one side border unit and mark it with a pin. From the pin in each direction, measure one-half the quilt length measurement and mark with pins. These marks correspond to the corner seam intersections on the quilt. Find center of quilt side by folding and mark it with a pin. Pin side border unit to quilt side, right sides together, matching corner seam intersections on quilt to corresponding marked points on border; match centers. Pin at intervals. Stitch, beginning and ending stitching at corner seam intersections. Repeat for other three borders.
3. Lay a corner of the quilt, right side up, on ironing board. The quilt may be pinned to the ironing board to keep it from falling

off or being distorted. With borders overlapping, fold one border under to a 45° angle. Match the seams or stripes and work with it until it matches perfectly. The outer edges should be very square and without any extra fullness. Seams and pattern lines should create a 90° angle. Press this fold.

4. Flip outside edge of border with pressed fold over to other outside edge of border, right sides together; pin along pressed fold. Stitch from inner corner (about ⅛″ from seamline) to outside of quilt. It may be helpful to baste this seam first. Check the seam for accuracy before stitching.
5. Lay mitered corner of quilt on ironing board right side up to see if stripes and seams match. Press. Trim mitered seam to ¼″.

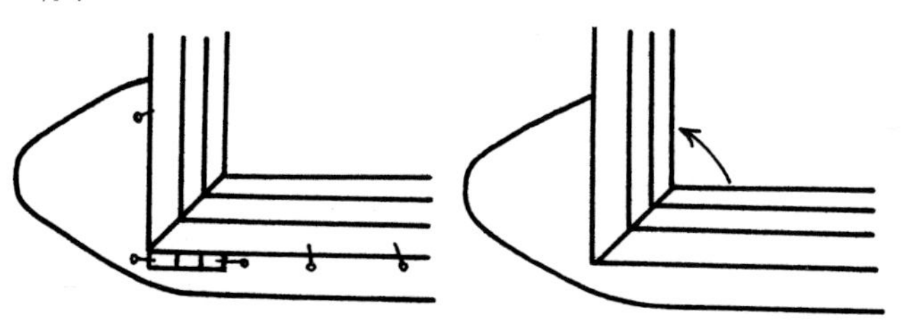

MARKING A QUILT TOP

1. If possible, mark quilting designs on the right side of the quilt top before layering it with backing and batting. It is much easier to work on a hard, flat surface.
2. Quilting designs can be taped to a sunny window. Hold quilt top in position over design and mark lightly with a pencil. Sometimes it is possible to mark quilting designs before quilt blocks are assembled which makes marking easier.
3. Many designs can be marked by making a template of the repeated shape. Be sure to make notches on template where the shapes overlap.
4. If using a stencil, mark lightly and carefully. Connect broken lines by marking freehand.
5. To mark for outline quilting, lay ¼″ masking tape along one side of seam, and then quilt next to the other edge of the tape. When finished quilting, simply pick up the strip of tape and reposition it for another quilting line.

PREPARATION OF BACKING AND BATTING

BACKING

1. Many quilt tops are wider than one width of fabric. Keep in mind that up to three widths of fabric may be necessary and that joining seams may run vertically *or* horizontally. Figure backing measurements on paper before cutting. Be sure to allow extra width and length over and above the size of the quilt top.
2. Tear or cut off selvages.
3. Stitch pieces together using ¼″ seam allowance. Press seams open, creating less bulk through which to quilt.

BATTING

1. If using prepackaged batting, choose the correct size needed, remembering to allow *at least* 2″ to 3″ extra around entire quilt.
2. Before using batting, open it out fully a day before it is needed. This allows batting to "relax". Most wrinkles and creases should disappear, making it easier to layer.
3. If using batting sold by the yard, it may be necessary to seam widths together. This is very easily done by butting the batting edges together (not overlapping) and securing them with large, fairly loose whipstitches. Whipstitch on both sides of batting. Take care when quilting not to pull seam apart.

BASTING

1. This step joins the three layers (quilt top, batting, and backing) together in preparation for quilting.
2. Layer the quilt backing, right side down, then the batting, and then the quilt top, right side up. Trim batting to same size as backing.
3. Thread basting is best for hand quilting projects. Use a long running stitch, catching the three layers every few inches. Start in the center and baste toward the edges in a sunburst design. Roll the backing and batting at the outer edges over to the front; baste in place with large stitches. This will protect the batting. As quilting stitches are added, basting stitches should be removed.

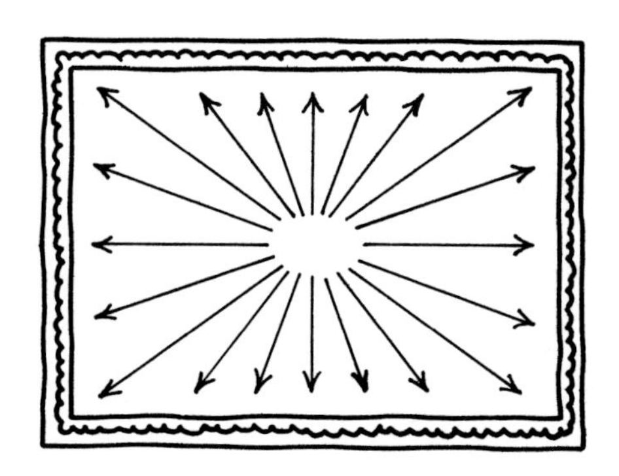

4. Pin basting can be done with one-inch safety pins if quilting will be done quickly so they can be removed before damaging quilt. This method works best for machine quilting. Place pins 4″ to 6″ apart, away from places where quilting lines will be. Edges can be rolled and pinned or left flat as desired.

HAND QUILTING

1. Hand quilting is a very tiny running stitch which creates a decorative pattern and holds all three layers of a quilt together. Use a single strand of quilting thread with a tiny knot at one end.
2. Insert quilting needle from the top through the quilt top and batting but not the backing; bring the needle up where the quilting line will begin. Gently tug knot so that it slips through the top layer and lodges in the batting.
3. Plant the needle point straight down and lodge the eye end of the needle in one of the thimble indentions, releasing the thumb and index finger. Placing the thumb on the quilt surface ahead of the needle point, and exerting a steady pressure on the needle with the thimble finger, stitch, rocking the needle up and down so as to take several stitches at one time. Make sure the needle is penetrating all layers by placing a finger of the other hand under the quilt where the needle penetrates.

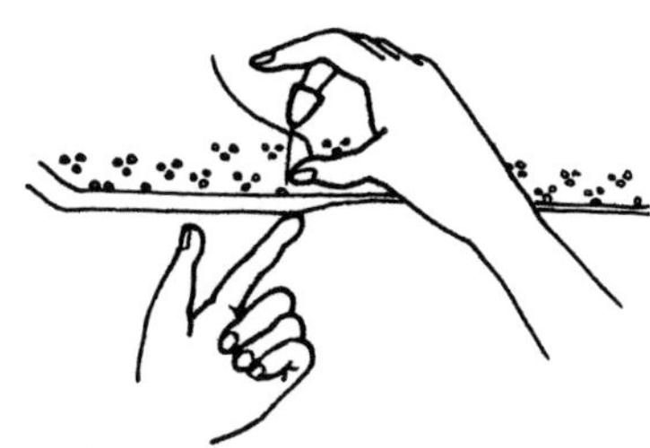

4. To end, make a knot that rests on the quilt top close to the last stitch; insert the needle a stitch length away and run it between the layers for a needle's length. Bring the needle back through the top and tug on the thread to pop the knot into the batting. Cut thread.
5. Outline quilting is quilting done ¼″ from seamlines. It avoids seams and shows up well. "Eyeball" the ¼″, use a pencil line, or quilt next to a piece of ¼″ masking tape. Remove tape when not quilting. Quilting "in the ditch" involves stitching very close to the seamline and is nearly invisible from the top of the quilt. Quilt on the side that does not have the seam allowance. It holds the layers together but does not add another design dimension to the quilt.

MACHINE QUILTING

1. Layer backing, batting and quilt top as in step 2 in basting section above. Pin baste with one-inch safety pins. Place pins other than where quilting lines will be as they are very difficult to remove while quilting.
2. Use an even-feed foot on the machine. Quilting should be at least every 6″. Some options are:
   a. Quilt in the ditch outlining blocks and/or sashings.
   b. Quilt in the ditch between patches every 4″ to 6″.
   c. Quilt straight, parallel lines either diagonally or vertically and horizontally by following some of the seams in the patchwork.
   d. Lay ¼″ masking tape down on the quilt top in desired places and stitch next to it.
   e. Mark top lightly with pencil and quilt on pencil line.
3. Use regular poly/cotton or 100% cotton thread on both the top of the sewing machine and in the bobbin or substitute fine transparent nylon thread for the top thread only. When not using nylon thread, it works best to use the same color thread on the top and in the bobbin.
4. Tightly roll the right side of the quilt to fit through the arm of the sewing machine. Provide support for the quilt to the left and behind the machine in the form of an extra table. If quilting parallel lines vertically and horizontally, for example,

work on the right half of the quilt first, starting at the edge near the center of the top or bottom border; then flip the quilt around 180° and work on the left half. Repeat for horizontal lines.

5. When sewing, hold the work flat with one hand on each side of the machine foot. Try to open the seam as much as possible so that when the slight tension is released, the stitching "disappears".

TYING

1. Layer backing, batting and quilt top as in step 2 in basting section above. Baste using pins or thread.
2. Use perle cotton, six strands of embroidery floss, ⅛″ ribbon, fingering yarn, or fine crochet cotton and a darning needle to tie quilt.
3. Tie quilt at 4″ to 6″ intervals, working from the center out.
4. Poke the needle through all layers and come up approximately ⅛″ away. Take an identical stitch directly on top of the first one. Move to the next spot.
5. Repeat step 4 until thread runs out. Rethread and continue until whole quilt is caught with these stitches.
6. Clip threads between stitches.
7. Tie a square knot at each point. Trim thread ends.

BINDING

A double binding is recommended because of its durability. Bias strips are not needed unless binding must go around a curve.

1. Piece ends of 2½″ wide strips to fit each side of quilt. Press the binding in half lengthwise, wrong sides together.
2. Put binding strips on in the same order the borders were added, usually the side pieces first and then the top and bottom pieces.
3. To apply, pin binding to opposite edges of quilt, pinning on the right side and having raw edges even. Stitch, using a ⅜″ seam allowance and, if possible, use an even-feed foot to prevent binding from "scooting " ahead. Bring binding over the raw edge so that the fold of the binding meets the stitched line on the back. Pin binding in place on back at four corners.
4. Pin and then stitch binding to remaining edges of quilt as above, except allow the binding to extend ½″ at both ends. Turn the extended portion of the binding in before turning the binding to the back. Handstitch binding to back of quilt at stitched line.

THE QUILTS

Let's make a personalized token of love for a special baby. The following charts include yardage requirements for cradle or doll size, crib size and twin size quilts. Read the charts and directions thoroughly before proceeding. Directions include a scale drawing of the CRIB size quilt and diagrams for piecing the block. Refer to *Glossary of Techniques* for help with specific quiltmaking methods.

Because of fabric shrinkage, cutting techniques and individual cutting discrepancies, the yardage for these quilts has been adjusted upwards. It is always a good idea to cut the entire quilt as soon as possible so that more fabric can be purchased if necessary. Extra fabric is included for quilts with mitered borders. Border and binding fabric have generally been listed separately from fabric specified for patchwork. This allows for individual choices. Measurements are given width × length. Border width and styles may vary for different sizes of the same quilt (i.e., pieced borders on cradle quilts may be eliminated due to size restrictions). Measure *your* quilt before cutting borders. Check quilt diagrams to see which border to stitch on first.

FINISHING STEPS FOR ALL QUILTS: See *Glossary of Techniques* for more detailed descriptions.

1. Press quilt top well.
2. Mark quilt for quilting if desired.
3. If necessary (depending on size), piece backing and batting together. Backings may be pieced horizontally or vertically. See cutting directions.
4. Layer backing, batting and quilt top; baste.
5. Quilt by hand or machine, or tie.
6. Bind quilt.

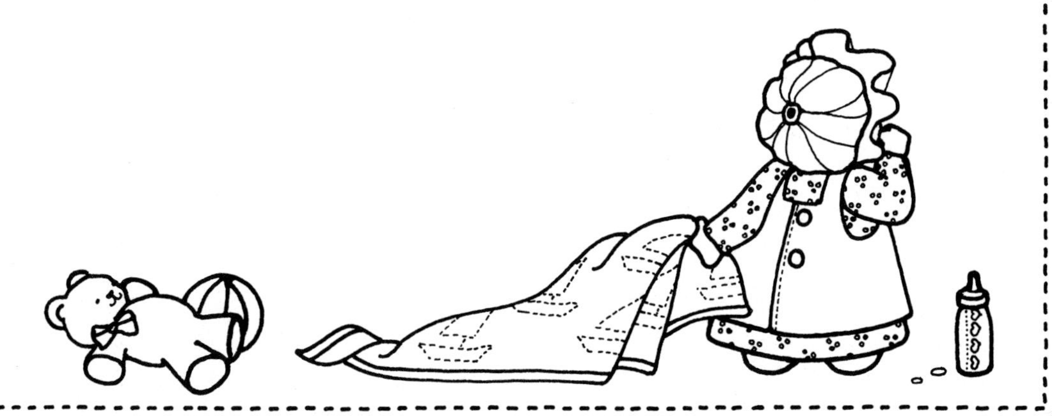

A TASKET, A TISKET

BLOCK SIZE: 2½″
SETTING: Squares—pleated, stitched and stuffed to make puffy biscuits.

	TEMPLATE OR CUT SIZE	CRADLE	CRIB	TWIN
APPROXIMATE FINISHED SIZE		30″ × 40″	40″ × 55″	70″ × 102″
BLOCKS SET		12 × 16	16 × 22	28 × 41
TOTAL NUMBER OF BLOCKS		192	352	1148
YARDAGE (42″-45″ width):				
Scraps of fabric at least 5″ square to total		3¼ yds.	5⅞ yds.	18½ yds.
Binding		⅜ yd.	½ yd.	¾ yd.
Backing (pieced vertically)		1⅓ yds.	1¾ yds.	6¼ yds.
Polyester fiberfill		1#	1-2#	3-4#
CUTTING:				
Scraps	J	192	352	1148
Binding	2½″ × fabric width	4 strips	5 strips	9 strips

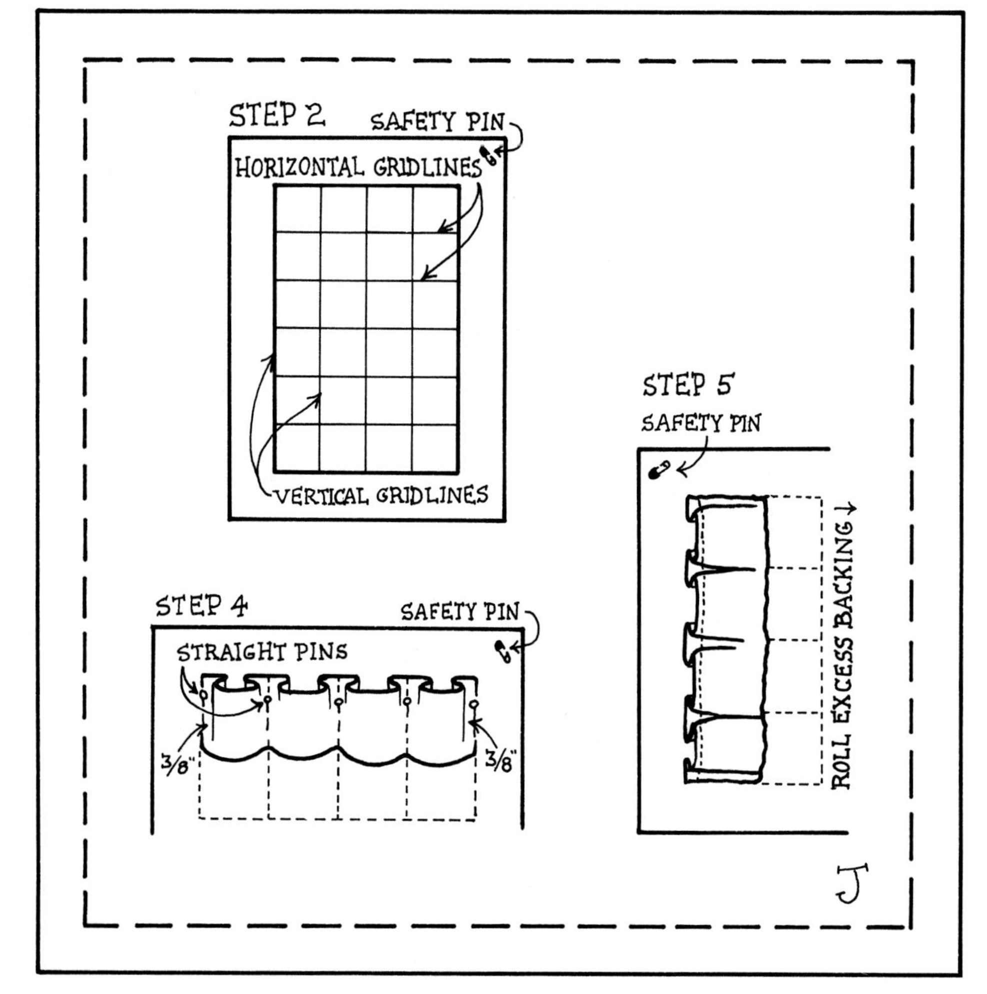

DIRECTIONS: Use ¼″ seams throughout. Refer to *Glossary of Techniques* for specific methods. Follow quilt diagram and add or subtract blocks to obtain desired size.

1. Piece and trim backing, if necessary, to be approximately 2″ to 4″ bigger than finished size of quilt. Press seams open. (Cradle and crib size need to be trimmed to size only.)
2. On wrong side of backing, center and draw grid of 2½″ squares with a pencil to equal number of blocks for desired size of quilt (i.e., crib grid = 16 squares × 22 squares). Mark top right corner of gridded backing with safety pin.
3. Randomly piece the 5″ squares into strips: Cradle = 12, Crib = 16, Twin = 28. Press seams to one side.
4. Place one strip on gridded backing, wrong sides together, along top edge, raw edge of strip on first horizontal gridline. Pin seams to vertical gridlines. Pin tucks at corners of each square. Start with first tuck ⅜″ from cut end of strip and end with last tuck ⅜″ from cut end of strip.
5. With bulk of backing to right, and safety pin at top left, sew strip to backing along first horizontal gridline, sewing down tucks at corners of each square. It is easiest to roll the gridded backing to fit it into the sewing machine.
6. Finish pinning seamlines between blocks of strip to vertical gridlines on backing, working in the excess which will be tucked later.
7. Lightly stuff each biscuit.
8. Sew open side of strip, wrong sides together, to second horizontal gridline on backing, creating tucks as before. Do not tuck under the raw edge.
9. Place a second strip, right sides together, onto the previous, tucked strip. Sew, creating tucks as before. Turn strip right side up and pin seamlines as before. Stuff each biscuit lightly.
10. Continue adding strips, pinning between blocks and stuffing until grid is covered.
11. Sew on vertical gridlines by removing one pin at a time and creating tucks as before. Stuff, tuck and sew both open side edges first. Keep bulk of quilt to left of machine.
12. Trim away excess backing along outer gridlines even with cut edges of biscuits.
13. Bind following directions given in *Glossary of Techniques*.

A TASKET, A TISKET (A Green and Yellow Biscuit) by Jane Dumler, 1990, 40″ × 55″. A reproduced collection of 1930's prints sets off this cuddly puff quilt made with a new method entirely on the machine.

BABY TEARS

BLOCK SIZE: 3″
SETTING: Four-patch blocks alternating with plain squares set on point.

	TEMPLATE OR CUT SIZE	CRADLE	CRIB	TWIN
APPROXIMATE FINISHED SIZE		28″ × 32″	49″ × 62″	68″ × 102″
BLOCKS SET		5 × 6	10 × 13	14 × 22
TOTAL NUMBER OF BLOCKS		30 pieced	130 pieced	308 pieced
YARDAGE (42″-45″ width):				
Muslin		1¼ yds.	3⅛ yds.	6½ yds.
Pink print (all same) *or*		¼ yd.	⅞ yd.	1⅞ yds.
small prints		⅛ yd. each of 5	⅙ yd. each of 10	¼ yd. each of 14
Ribbon roses (optional)		20	108	273
Binding		⅜ yd.	½ yd.	¾ yd.
Backing (pieced vertically)		1⅛ yds.	3⅞ yds.	6¼ yds.
Batting (48″ width)		1 yd.	3¾ yds.	6 yds.
Batting (prepackaged)		45″ × 60″	72″ × 90″	90″ × 108″
CUTTING:				
Muslin	Z	20	108	273
	D	60	260	616
	a	18	42	68
	b	4	4	4
One print (all blocks the same)	D	60	260	616
Many prints	D	12 each of 5	26 each of 10	44 each of 14
Borders—( )= # of strips to cut				
Border—Cradle & Crib				
Sides	3½″ wide	× 26″ (2)	× 55¾″ (3)	
Top & bottom	3½″ wide	× 27¾″ (2)	× 49″ (3)	
Border—Twin				
Sides	4½″ wide			× 94″ (5)
Top & bottom	4½″ wide			× 68″ (4)
Binding	2½″ × fabric width	3 strips	6 strips	9 strips

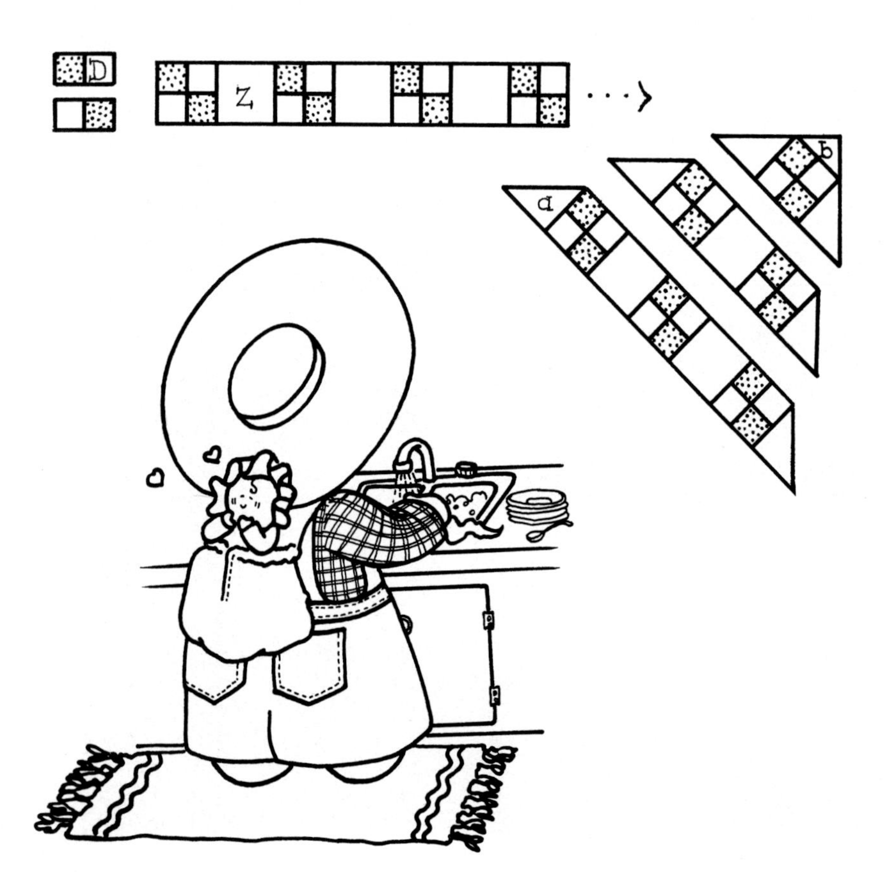

DIRECTIONS: Use ¼″ seams throughout. Refer to *Glossary of Techniques* for specific methods. Follow quilt diagram and add or subtract blocks to obtain desired size.

1. Piece 4-patch blocks following diagram.
2. Piece diagonal rows alternating with plain blocks.
3. Add small triangles to rows that go to corners. Add large triangles to other rows. See quilt diagram.
4. Piece rows together following quilt diagram.
5. For border, follow cutting directions and stitch strips together, if necessary, to make the needed lengths. Add border by sewing on sides first then top and bottom.
6. Refer to *Finishing Steps For All Quilts* on page 15. Machine quilt in the ditch or outline quilt small squares by hand and quilt a heart in each large square. Interlocking hearts are quilted in border. Quilting design is on page 75. See diagram for placement of quilting design at sides of quilt. Tack ribbon roses to centers of large squares, if desired, instead of quilting the hearts.

QUILTING DESIGN PLACEMENT

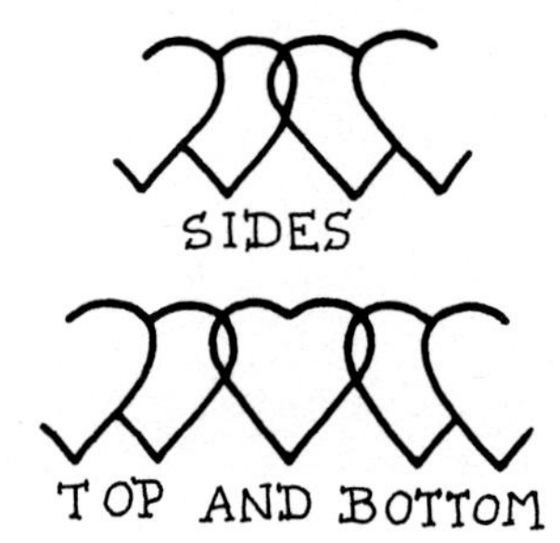

BABY TEARS by Nancy Smith, quilted by Gwenn Michal and Sharon Holmes, 1990, 28″ × 32″. Left plain and simple or decorated in a variety of beautiful ways, this quilt can be used to soothe a baby's tears. It is also reminiscent of the colorful strings of beads we all enjoyed as babies.

BIBS N' BONNETS

BLOCK SIZE: 8″
SETTING: Blocks are set straight, alternating boys with girls, set with sashing strips and setting squares. Pieced border on crib and twin sizes only.

	TEMPLATE OR CUT SIZE	CRADLE	CRIB	TWIN
APPROXIMATE FINISHED SIZE		28″ × 38″	54″ × 63″	66″ × 105″
BLOCKS SET		2 × 3	4 × 5	5 × 9
TOTAL NUMBER OF BLOCKS		6	20	45
YARDAGE (42″-45″ width):				
Muslin-setting squares, background & borders		1¼ yds.	2⅝ yds.	5⅛ yds.
Floral-sashing strips and border		½ yd. (no border)	1½ yds.	2¾ yds.
Scraps for applique (3 fabrics per block) *or*		18 - 6′ × 6″	60 - 6″ × 6″	135 - 6″ × 6″
scraps to total		½ yd.	1¾ yds.	4 yds.
Scraps for border squares to total		NA	½ yd.	¾ yd.
Flesh solid—faces & hands		⅛ yd.	⅛ yd.	¼ yd.
Tan—shoes		⅛ yd.	⅛ yd.	¼ yd.
Binding		⅜ yd.	½ yd.	¾ yd.
Backing (pieced vertically)		1¼ yds.	3⅞ yds.	6⅜ yds.
Batting (48″ width)		1 yd.	3¾ yds.	6¼ yds.
Batting (prepackaged)		45″ × 60″	72″ × 90″	90″ × 108″
Embroidery floss				
CUTTING (except applique pieces):				
Muslin-background squares	d	6	20	45
setting squares	C	12	30	60
Floral sashing strips	s	17	49	104
Borders—( )= # of strips to cut				
Border—Cradle				
Sides	3½″ wide	× 32½″ (2)		
Top & bottom	3½″ wide	× 28½″ (2)		
Border 1—Crib				
Sides	3½″ wide		× 52½″ (3)	
Top & bottom	3″ wide		× 48½″ (3)	
Border 1—Twin				
Sides	4½″ wide			× 92½″ (5)
Top & bottom	4″ wide			× 60½″ (4)
Border 2—Crib & Twin				
Muslin triangles	E		4	4
Muslin triangles	b		70	106
Scrap print squares	r		74	110
Floral triangles	b		70	106
Floral triangles	E		12	12
Binding	2½″ × fabric width	4 strips	6 strips	9 strips

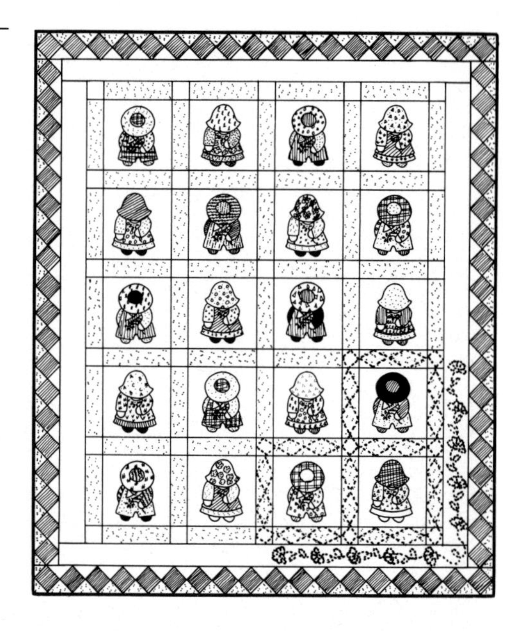

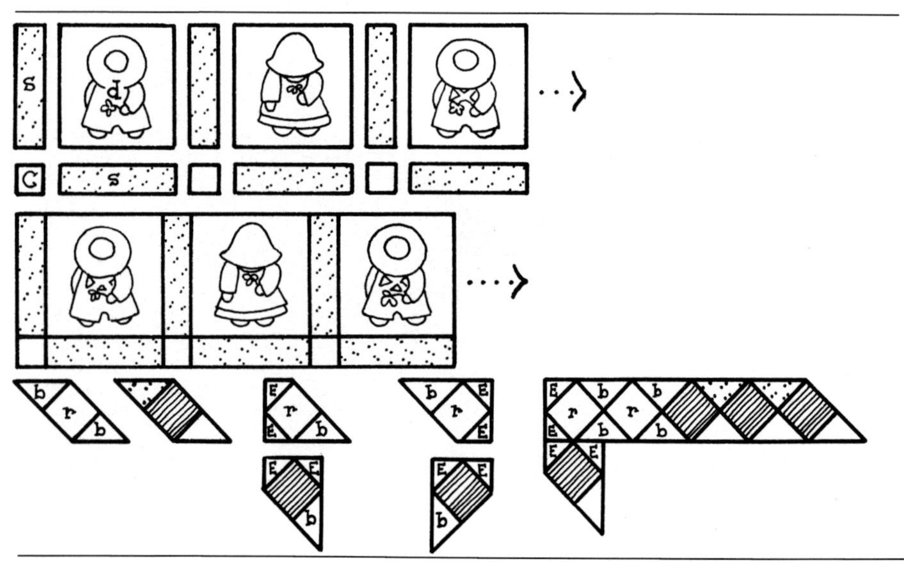

DIRECTIONS: Use ¼″ seams throughout. Refer to *Glossary of Techniques* for specific methods. Follow quilt diagram and add or subtract blocks to obtain desired size.

1. Prepare appliques referring to *Glossary of Techniques.*
2. Position applique pieces on background squares using centering guide on pattern. Baste.
3. Applique pieces using thread that matches each fabric as closely as possible.
4. Stitch finished blocks to sashing strips using quilt diagram as a guide.
5. Stitch setting squares to sashing strips to create horizontal rows of pieced sashing.
6. Stitch rows of blocks and rows of sashing together alternately.
7. For first border, follow cutting directions and stitch strips together, if necessary, to make the needed lengths. Stitch first border to quilt sides first then top and bottom.
8. Following diagram, stitch squares and triangles together for side border. Stitch onto quilt.
9. Stitch squares and triangles together for top and bottom borders. Stitch onto quilt.
10. Refer to *Finishing Steps For All Quilts* on page 15. Applique pieces are outline quilted on muslin background and in the ditch on applique pieces. Background squares are stitched in the ditch. Sashing strips and setting squares are quilted in a diamond design, and a daisy chain is quilted in the first border. Quilting designs are on page 73. The second border is outline quilted.

BIBS N' BONNETS designed by Nancy Smith and Lynda Milligan, pieced and appliqued by Terri Wiley, hand quilted by Saloma Yoder, 1989, 54″ × 63″. This new version of Overall Bill and Sunbonnet Sue offers a family of friends to that special someone. For *Baby Tears* quilt, see page 18.

CUDDLE UP

BLOCK SIZE: Approx. 4¼″
SETTING: Blocks are straight set alternating pink and blue centers. Yardage allows extra for quick cutting technique.

	TEMPLATE OR CUT SIZE	CRADLE	CRIB	TWIN
APPROXIMATE FINISHED SIZE		30″ × 39″	43″ × 60″	69″ × 103″
BLOCKS SET		5 × 7	8 × 12	14 × 22
TOTAL NUMBER OF BLOCKS		35	96	308
YARDAGE (42″-45″ width):				
Light pink scraps to total		¼ yd.	½ yd.	1½ yds.
Light blue scraps to total		¼ yd.	½ yd.	1½ yds.
Medium pink scraps to total		½ yd.	1¼ yds.	3¾ yds.
Medium blue scraps to total		½ yd.	1¼ yds.	3¾ yds.
Pink & blue stripe for border		⅜ yd.	½ yd.	¾ yd.
Blue for border		⅝ yd.	¾ yd.	1¼ yds.
Binding		⅜ yd.	½ yd.	¾ yd.
Backing (pieced vertically)		1⅓ yds.	3¾ yds.	6¼ yds.
Batting (48″ width)		1 yd.	1⅞ yds.	6 yds.
Batting (prepackaged)		45″ × 60″	72″ × 90″	90″ × 108″
CUTTING:				
Light pink scraps	Z	17	48	154
Light blue scraps	Z	18	48	154
Medium pink scraps	b or 2¼″ wide strips	72	192	616
Medium blue scraps	b or 2¼″ wide strips	68	192	616
Borders—( )= # of strips to cut				
Border 1				
Sides	2″ wide	× 35″ (2)	× 47″ (3)	× 75″ (4)
Top & bottom	2″ wide	× 43″ (3)	× 64″ (3)	× 109″ (6)
Border 2				
Sides	3½″ wide	× 35″ (2)	× 47″ (3)	× 75″ (4)
Top & bottom	3½″ wide	× 43″ (3)	× 64″ (3)	× 109″ (6)
Binding	2½″ × fabric width	4 strips	6 strips	9 strips

TRADITIONAL METHOD

PINEAPPLE RULE METHOD

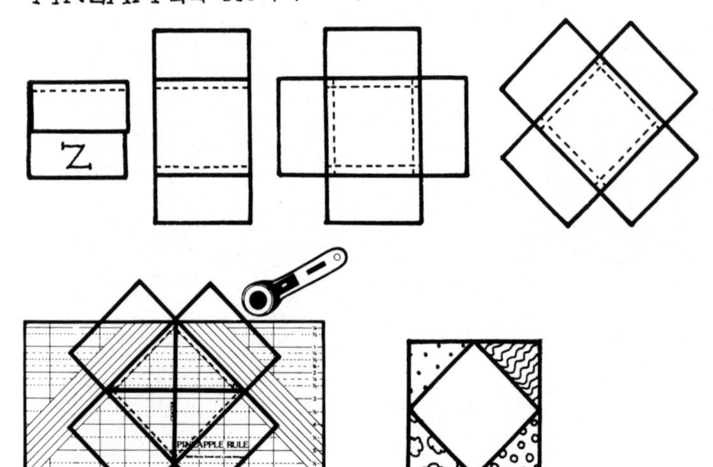

DIRECTIONS: Use ¼″ seams throughout. Refer to *Glossary of Techniques* for specific methods. Follow quilt diagram and add or subtract blocks to obtain desired size.

1. For traditional piecing, sew b triangles onto Z squares. Blue triangles are usually pieced around pink squares and pink triangles around blue squares, but reverse as desired.
2. For Pineapple Rule method, sew 2¼″ wide strips around each square as illustrated.
3. Place Pineapple Rule on wrong side of block with 45° angles following stitching lines. The center vertical line should match point to point with the square. Using rotary cutter, trim off corners as shown. Swing block 90° and repeat this process three more times.
4. Piece blocks together to form rows, alternating pink-cornered squares with blue-cornered squares.
5. Piece rows together following quilt diagram.
6. For borders, follow cutting directions and stitch strips together, if necessary, to make the needed lengths.
7. Stitch borders to quilt and miter corners.
8. Refer to *Finishing Steps For All Quilts* on page 15. Quilt is machine quilted in the ditch.

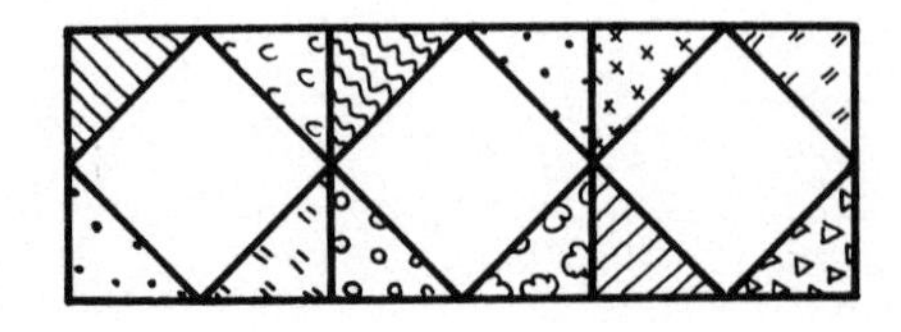

CUDDLE UP by Lynda Milligan, machine quilted by Sharon Holmes, 1990, 43″ × 60″. This scrap quilt can be made using the quick-piecing "Pineapple Rule" technique or traditional methods. Either way it is bound to be a favorite of "patchwork" lovers.

DAISY DAISY

BLOCK SIZE: 10½″
SETTING: Log cabin blocks set in straight furrows pattern with patchwork border.

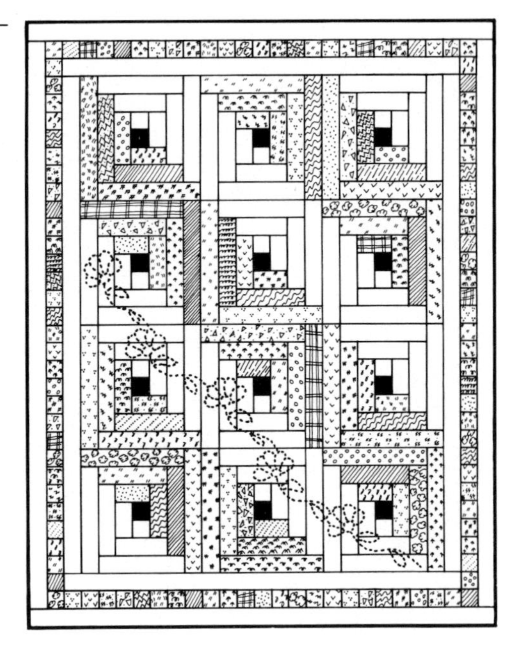

	TEMPLATE OR CUT SIZE	CRADLE	CRIB	TWIN
APPROXIMATE FINISHED SIZE		30″ × 41″	41″ × 51″	68″ × 99″
BLOCKS SET		2 × 3	3 × 4	5 × 8
TOTAL NUMBER OF BLOCKS		6	12	40
YARDAGE (42″-45″ width):				
Note: If using the strip method of log cabin, add a little extra to yardages.				
Muslin for blocks and borders		1¼ yds.	1⅝ yds.	4¾ yds.
Pink solid for center squares		⅛ yd.	⅛ yd.	¼ yd.
Scraps to total		1⅛ yds.	1⅝ yds.	4 yds.
Binding		⅜ yd.	½ yd.	¾ yd.
Backing (pieced vertically)		1⅜ yds.	3¼ yds.	6⅛ yds.
Batting (48″ width)		1 yd.	1⅝ yds.	6 yds.
Batting (prepackaged)		45″ × 60″	45″ × 60″	90″ × 108″
CUTTING:				
Pink center square	D	6	12	40
Muslin	D, i, j	6 of each	12 of each	40 of each
	k, l, m	6 of each	12 of each	40 of each
Prints	i, j, k	6 of each	12 of each	40 of each
	l, m, n	6 of each	12 of each	40 of each
Borders—( )= # of strips to cut				
Border 1—Cradle & Crib				
Sides	2″ wide	× 32″ (2)	× 42½″ (2)	
Top & bottom	2″ wide	× 24½″ (2)	× 35″ (2)	
Border 2—Cradle & Crib	D	82	110	
Border 3—Cradle & Crib				
Sides	2″ wide	× 38″ (2)	× 48½″ (3)	
Top & bottom	2″ wide	× 30½″ (2)	× 41″ (2)	
Border 1—Twin				
Sides	3½″ wide			× 84½″ (4)
Top & bottom	3½″ wide			× 59″ (3)
Border 2—Twin	D			202
Border 3—Twin				
Sides	3½″ wide			× 93½″ (5)
Top & bottom	3½″ wide			× 68″ (4)
Binding	2½″ × fabric width	4 strips	5 strips	9 strips

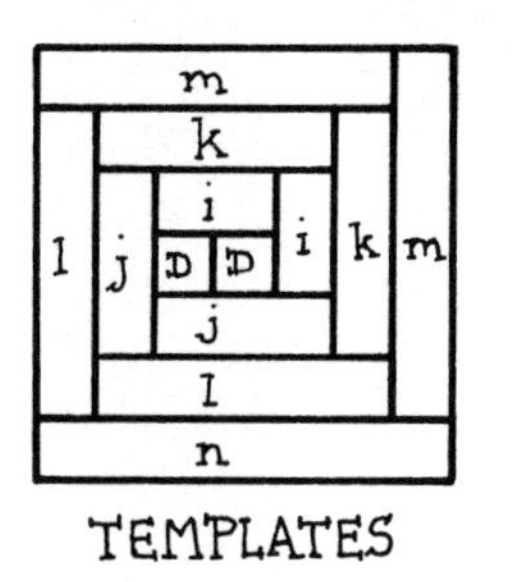

TEMPLATES

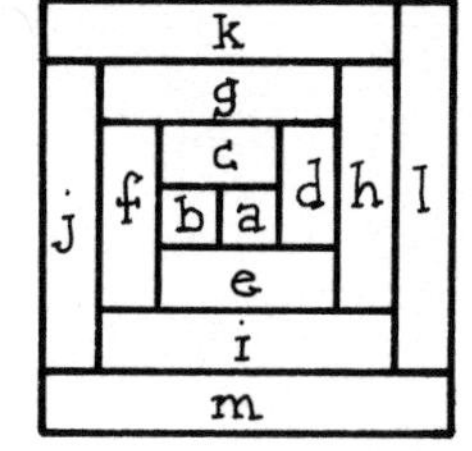

PIECING ORDER

DIRECTIONS: Use ¼″ seams throughout. Refer to *Glossary of Techniques* for specific methods. Follow quilt diagram and add or subtract blocks to obtain desired size. There are many ways to piece log cabin blocks. This method uses templates.

1. Referring to *Glossary of Techniques* and illustration, piece blocks following alphabetical sequence, starting with the muslin side and adding strips in a clockwise direction.
2. Sew blocks into chosen design by sewing blocks into rows first. Our sample is made in a straight furrow design.
3. For first and third borders, follow cutting directions and stitch strips together, if necessary, to make the needed lengths. Add first border, stitching sides on first then top and bottom.
4. Piece squares together for second border. Seven squares should fit along each log cabin square. Add pieced border to quilt sides first then top and bottom.
5. Add third border to quilt, stitching sides on first then top and bottom.
6. Refer to *Finishing Steps For All Quilts* on page 15. Quilt is machine quilted in the ditch around print strips. Large daisies are quilted by hand through muslin areas. Quilting design is on page 76.

DAISY DAISY by Nancy Smith, quilted by Sharon Holmes and Gwenn Michal, 1990, 41″ × 51″. The straight furrow set has been chosen for this appealing log cabin quilt. Enticing color schemes can be created using accumulated scraps.

GARDEN SONG

BLOCK SIZE: 10″

SETTING: Blocks are straight set with sashing strips and setting squares that form a secondary monkey wrench pattern.

	TEMPLATE OR CUT SIZE	CRADLE	CRIB	TWIN
APPROXIMATE FINISHED SIZE		30″ × 42″	46″ × 58″	70″ × 106″
BLOCKS SET		2 × 3	3 × 4	5 × 8
TOTAL NUMBER OF BLOCKS		6	12	40
YARDAGE (42″-45″ width):				
Muslin for blocks and sashing		1¼ yds.	2¼ yds.	5 yds.
Scraps to total		¾ yd.	1½ yds.	4½ yds.
Green		⅜ yd.	½ yd.	1¼ yds.
Border with seams		⅜ yd.	1 yd.	1½ yds.
Border without seams		1⅜ yds.	1⅞ yds.	3¼ yds.
Binding		⅜ yd.	½ yd.	¾ yd.
Backing (pieced vertically)		1⅜ yds.	3⅝ yds.	6⅜ yds.
Batting (48″ width)		1 yd.	1¾ yds.	6¼ yds.
Batting (prepackaged)		45″ × 60″	72″ × 90″	90″ × 108″
CUTTING:				
Muslin centers	N	6	12	40
Diamonds	L	48	96	320
Sashing strips	h	17	31	93
Setting squares	C	10	14	26
Scraps—petals	K	48	96	320
Green—corners of blocks	M	24	48	160
Setting squares	C	2	6	28
Borders—( )= # of strips to cut				
Border—Cradle				
Sides	2½″ wide	× 46″ (3)		
Top & bottom	2½″ wide	× 34″ (2)		
Border—Crib & Twin				
Sides	4½″ wide		× 62″ (4)	× 112″ (6)
Top & bottom	4½″ wide		× 50″ (3)	× 76″ (4)
Binding	2½″ × fabric width	4 strips	6 strips	9 strips

DIRECTIONS: Use ¼″ seams throughout. Refer to *Glossary of Techniques* for specific methods. Follow quilt diagram and add or subtract blocks to obtain desired size.

1. Piece blocks following diagram.
2. Baste ¼″ seam allowance under on circles. Keeping block as flat as possible, applique circles into place. It will help to fold circles into quarters and match with seamlines.
3. Piece blocks into rows with sashing strips.
4. Piece rows of setting squares and sashing strips together. Be aware of color changes in setting squares; all outside edge setting squares are muslin.
5. Stitch alternating rows of blocks and pieced sashing.
6. For borders, follow cutting directions and stitch strips together, if necessary, to make the needed lengths.
7. Attach borders and miter corners.
8. Refer to *Finishing Steps For All Quilts* on page 15. The blocks are outline quilted, and a flower and vine design is quilted in the sashing strips. Quilting design is on page 75.

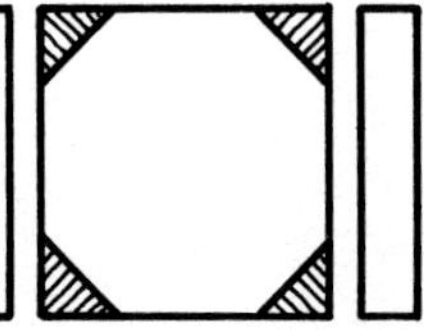

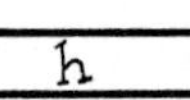

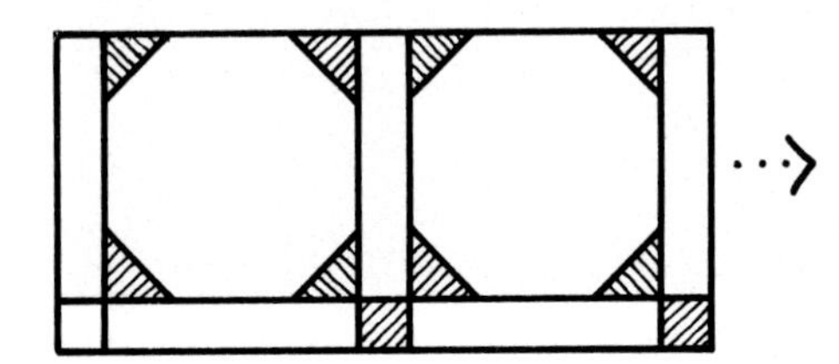

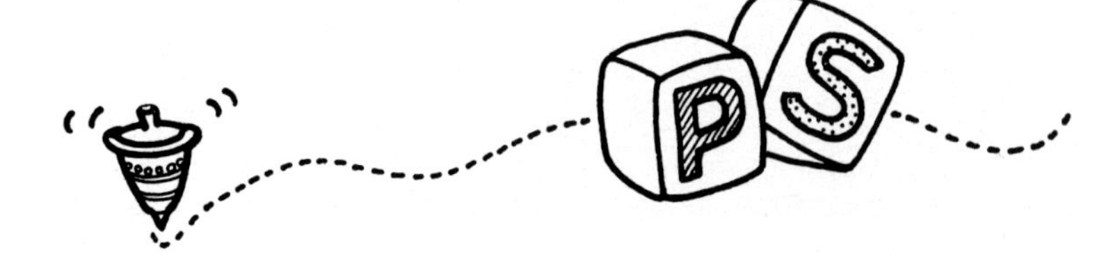

GARDEN SONG by Nancy Smith, hand quilted by Gwenn Michal, 1990, 46″ × 58″. What child would not delight in this garden collection of soft and appealing petals—a perfect pattern for gathering the scraps of friends or projects past.

HEART OF MY HEART

BLOCK SIZE: 7½″
SETTING: Pieced and appliqued fans set on point.

	TEMPLATE OR CUT SIZE	CRADLE	CRIB	TWIN
APPROXIMATE FINISHED SIZE		31″ × 42″	42″ × 53″	70″ × 102″
BLOCKS SET		2 × 3	3 × 4	5 × 8
TOTAL NUMBER OF BLOCKS		8	18	68
YARDAGE (42″-45″ width):				
Muslin for background		1⅛ yds.	1¾ yds.	4⅝ yds.
Pink solid		¼ yd.	⅜ yd.	1 yd.
Pink prints (5)		⅛ yd. each	¼ yd. each	¾ yd. each
First border		⅜ yd.	½ yd.	1 yd.
Second border		⅝ yd.	⅝ yd.	1¾ yds.
Binding		⅜ yd.	½ yd.	¾ yd.
Backing (pieced vertically)		1⅜ yds.	3⅜ yds.	6¼ yds.
Batting (48″ width)		1 yd.	1⅝ yds.	6 yds.
Batting (prepackaged)		45″ × 60″	45″ × 60″	90″ × 108″
CUTTING:				
Background—squares	o	8	18	68
large setting triangles	p	6	10	22
corner setting triangles	q	4	4	4
Pink solid—hearts	W	8	18	68
Pink prints (5)	V	8 of each	18 of each	68 of each
Borders—( )= # of strips to cut				
Border 1—Cradle & Crib				
Top & bottom	2½″ wide	× 21¾″ (2)	× 32⅜″ (2)	
Sides	2½″ wide	× 36⅜″ (2)	× 47″ (3)	
Border 2—Cradle & Crib				
Top & bottom	3½″ wide	× 25¾″ (2)	× 36⅜″ (2)	
Sides	3½″ wide	× 42⅜″ (3)	× 53″ (3)	
Border 1—Twin				
Top & bottom	3½″ wide			× 53⅝″ (3)
Sides	3½″ wide			× 91½″ (5)
Border 2—Twin				
Top & bottom	6″ wide			× 59⅝″ (5)
Sides	6″ wide			× 102½″ (5)
Binding	2½″ × fabric width	4 strips	5 strips	9 strips

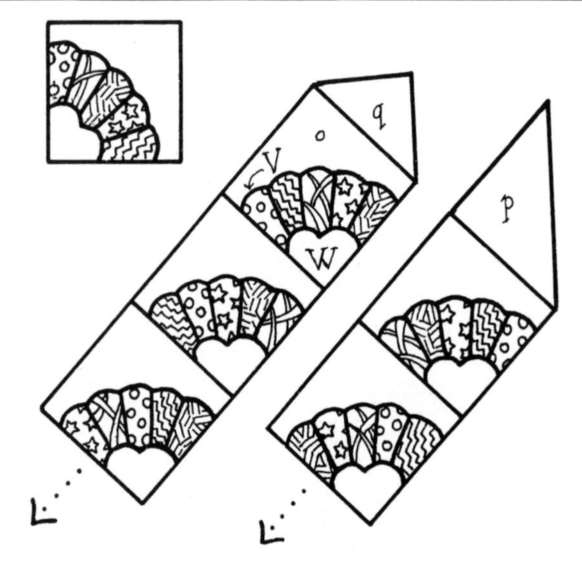

DIRECTIONS: Use ¼″ seams throughout. Refer to *Glossary of Techniques* for specific methods. Follow quilt diagram and add or subtract blocks to obtain desired size.

1. Piece five fan segments (V) together for each block.
2. Make a plastic template of the fan segment (V) without seam allowance. Lay template on the right side of each fan segment matching edges of template with seams. Trace curved edge to mark turn-under line for applique. Baste curved edge under on line.
3. Baste fans in place on background blocks (o), lining up raw straight edges of fan with raw edges of block.
4. Make a plastic template of heart (W). **A seam allowance is included on the straight edges but not on the curved edge.** Draw around template on right side of fabric. Cut out heart on straight solid lines but cut ¼″ from curved edge.
5. Baste curved edges under on heart.
6. Baste heart in place on block with straight edges even with raw edges of block.
7. Applique top edges of heart and fan segments with matching thread.
8. Carefully cut out excess muslin and prints from behind heart.
9. Following quilt diagram, piece blocks together into diagonal rows. Add triangles (p, q) to finish out rows.
10. Sew rows together.

Continued on page 50.

HEART OF MY HEART by Lynda Milligan, hand quilted by Great American Quilters, 1990, 42″ × 53″. This new version of the fan pattern with a heart in the center is sure to become someone's most cherished possession.

LEMON MERINGUE

BLOCK SIZE: 4½″
SETTING: Nine-patch squares alternating with plain blocks.

	TEMPLATE OR CUT SIZE	CRADLE	CRIB	TWIN
APPROXIMATE FINISHED SIZE		31″ × 40″	40″ × 49″	67″ × 103″
BLOCKS SET		5 × 7	7 × 9	13 × 21
TOTAL NUMBER OF BLOCKS		35 (18 pieced)	63 (32 pieced)	273 (137 pieced)
YARDAGE (42″-45″ width):				
Multi-colored floral (D & J squares)		⅞ yd.	1¼ yds.	4⅜ yds.
Yellow (squares and border)		1 yd.	1¼ yds.	3⅝ yds.
Binding		⅜ yd.	½ yd.	¾ yd.
Backing (pieced vertically)		1⅜ yds.	3¼ yds.	6¼ yds
Batting (48″ width)		1 yd.	1½ yds.	6 yds.
Batting (prepackaged)		45″ × 60″	45″ × 60″	90″ × 108″
CUTTING:				
Multi-colored floral	D	72	128	548
	J	17	31	136
Yellow	D	90	160	685
Border—( )= # of strips to cut				
Sides	4¾″ wide	× 32″ (2)	× 41″ (2)	× 95″ (5)
Top & bottom	4¾″ wide	× 31½″ (2)	× 40½″ (2)	× 67½″ (4)
Binding	2½″ × fabric width	4 strips	5 strips	9 strips

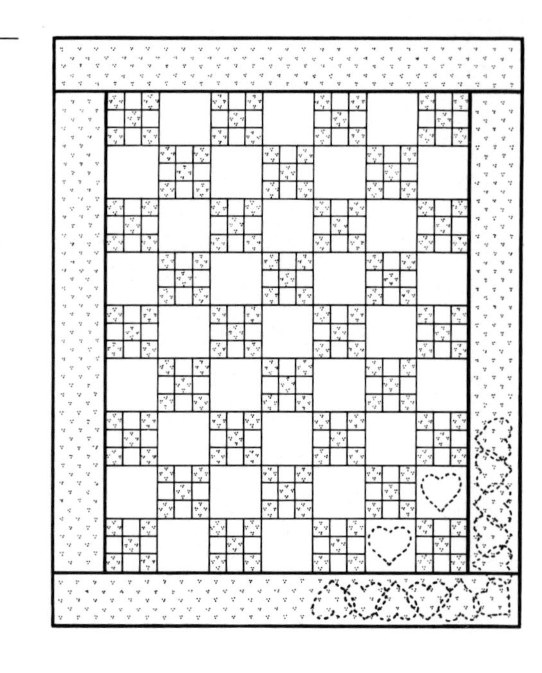

DOTTED LINE MAY BE NECESSARY FOR STRETCHING HEART TO FIT TOP & BOTTOM BORDERS.

QUILTING DESIGN

DIRECTIONS: Use ¼″ seams throughout. Refer to *Glossary of Techniques* for specific methods. Follow quilt diagram and add or subtract blocks to obtain desired size.

1. Piece blocks following diagram.
2. Piece horizontal rows following diagram.
3. Piece rows together following quilt diagram.
4. For border, follow cutting directions and stitch strips together, if necessary, to make the needed lengths.
5. Sew border to quilt sides first then top bottom.
6. Refer to *Finishing Steps For All Quilts* on page 15. Quilt is hand quilted in the ditch around all squares. Large square is quilted with a heart, and an interlocking heart is quilted in the borders.

LEMON MERINGUE by Lynda Milligan, hand quilted by Gwenn Michal, 1990, 41″ × 50″. This simplest of patterns, a nine-patch alternating with a plain block, can be masculine or feminine, bright or soft. A change in the quilting pattern can vary the mood and overall effect of the quilt.

LOLLIPOPS AND LEMONDROPS

BLOCK SIZE: 6″
SETTING: Straight set blocks with sashing and setting squares.

	TEMPLATE OR CUT SIZE	CRADLE	CRIB	TWIN
APPROXIMATE FINISHED SIZE		34″ × 42″	42″ × 50″	66″ × 106″
BLOCKS SET		4 × 5	5 × 6	8 × 13
TOTAL NUMBER OF BLOCKS		20	30	104
YARDAGE (42″-45″ width):				
Large floral (squares)		1 yd.	1⅛ yds.	3¾ yds.
Red stripe (sashing strips)		⅞ yd.	1⅛ yds.	3⅛ yds.
Red print (setting squares)		¼ yd.	⅜ yd.	⅞ yd.
Binding		⅜ yd.	½ yd.	¾ yd.
Backing (pieced vertically)		1⅜ yds.	3¼ yds.	6⅜ yds.
Batting (48″ width)		1⅛ yds.	1½ yds.	6¼ yds.
Batting (prepackaged)		45″ × 60″	45″ × 60″	90″ × 108″
CUTTING:				
Large floral squares	A	20	30	104
Red stripe sashing	B	49	71	229
Red print setting squares	C	30	42	126
Binding	2½″ × fabric width	4 strips	5 strips	9 strips

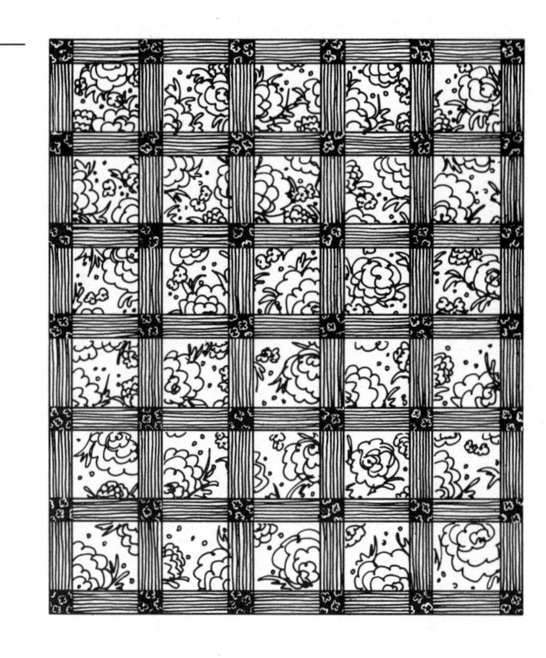

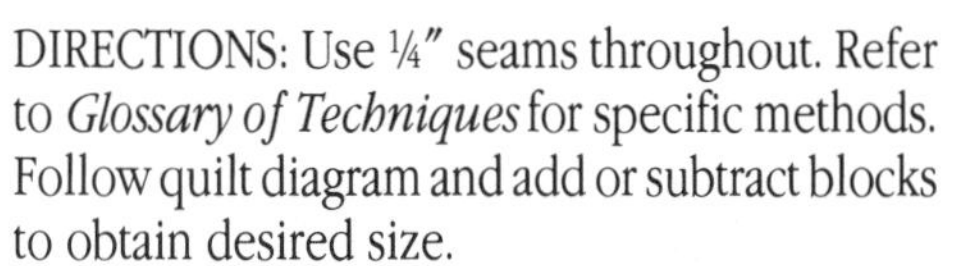

DIRECTIONS: Use ¼″ seams throughout. Refer to *Glossary of Techniques* for specific methods. Follow quilt diagram and add or subtract blocks to obtain desired size.

1. Piece horizontal rows of squares and sashing strips following diagram. Piece horizontal rows of setting squares and sashing strips.
2. Stitch alternating rows of blocks and pieced sashing.
3. Refer to *Finishing Steps For All Quilts* on page 15. Quilt is machine quilted in the ditch around each piece.

LOLLIPOPS AND LEMONDROPS by Nancy Smith, machine quilted by Sharon Holmes, 1990, 42″ × 50″. This simple, plain block set with strips can be used to showcase any special fabric from a whimsical print to a decorator floral.

LULLABY

BLOCK SIZE: 6″
SETTING: Pinwheels set straight with sashing and setting squares.

	TEMPLATE OR CUT SIZE	CRADLE	CRIB	TWIN
APPROXIMATE FINISHED SIZE		34″ × 42″	42″ × 50″	66″ × 106″
BLOCKS SET		4 × 5	5 × 6	8 × 13
TOTAL NUMBER OF BLOCKS		20	30	104
YARDAGE (42″-45″ width):				
Pink stripe		1 yd.	1¼ yds.	3¼ yds.
Blue print		¾ yd.	1⅛ yds.	3⅛ yds.
Medium pink print		½ yd.	⅝ yd.	1¾ yds.
Light pink print		½ yd.	⅝ yd.	1¾ yds.
Binding		⅜ yd.	½ yd.	¾ yd.
Backing (pieced vertically)		1⅜ yds.	3¼ yds.	6⅜ yds.
Batting (48″ width)		1⅛ yds.	1½ yds.	6¼ yds.
Batting (prepackaged)		45″ × 60″	45″ × 60″	90″ × 108″
CUTTING:				
Pink stripe-sashing strips	B	49	71	229
Blue print-setting squares	C	30	42	126
triangles	a	80	120	416
Medium pink print	b	80	120	416
Light pink print	b	80	120	416
Binding	2½″ × fabric width	4 strips	5 strips	9 strips

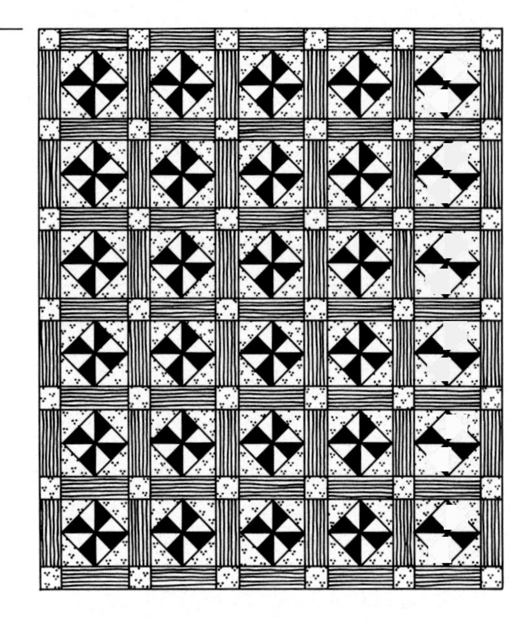

DIRECTIONS: Use ¼″ seams throughout. Refer to *Glossary of Techniques* for specific methods. Follow quilt diagram and add or subtract blocks to obtain desired size.

1. Piece blocks following diagram.
2. Piece horizontal rows alternating sashing strips with pieced blocks. Piece horizontal rows of setting squares and sashing strips.
3. Stitch alternating rows of blocks and pieced sashing.
4. Refer to *Finishing Steps For All Quilts* on page 15. Quilt is machine quilted in the ditch around each pinwheel and next to setting strips and squares.

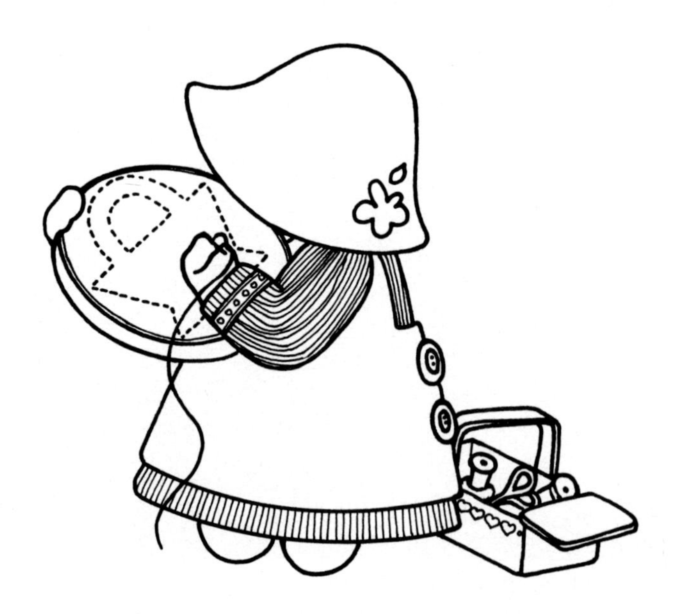

LULLABY by Nancy Smith, machine quilted by Sharon Holmes, 1990, 42″ × 50″. This traditional, easy-to-piece pinwheel pattern, set on point, is presented in soft, appealing colors. The combination of pinks and blues makes it especially suitable for either a boy or girl.

PINWHEELS

BLOCK SIZE: 7″
SETTING: Straight set, block to block. Cradle does not include pieced border.

	TEMPLATE OR CUT SIZE	CRADLE	CRIB	TWIN
APPROXIMATE FINISHED SIZE		33″ × 40″	46″ × 58″	67″ × 104″
BLOCKS SET		4 × 5	4 × 6	7 × 13
TOTAL NUMBER OF BLOCKS		20	24	91
YARDAGE (42″-45″ width):				
Muslin for background and borders		1⅜ yds.	3 yds.	6⅜ yds.
Multi-colored floral		1 yd.	1¼ yds.	2¾ yds.
Small prints		⅙ yd. ea. of 5	¼ yd. each of 6	½ yd. each of 7
Binding		⅜ yd.	½ yd.	¾ yd.
Backing (pieced vertically)		1⅓ yds.	3⅝ yds.	6¼ yds.
Batting (48″ width)		1 yd.	1¾ yds.	6 yds.
Batting (prepackaged)		45″ × 60″	72″ × 90″	90″ × 108″
CUTTING:				
Muslin				
Pinwheel triangles	F	80	96	364
Pinwheel trapezoids	G	80	96	364
Border triangles	H		84	152
Border 3-squares	C		4	4
Multi-colored floral				
Pinwheel triangles	F	80	96	364
Border triangles	H		44	76
Small prints				
Pinwheels	F	16 each of 5	16 each of 6	52 each of 7
Border triangles	H		7 each of 6	11 each of 7
Borders—Please pay close attention to sizes. Widths may vary in order for sawtooth border to fit accurately. Cradle includes first two borders only, no sawtooth.				
Borders—( )= # of strips to cut				
Border 1—Cradle				
Sides	1″ wide	× 35½″ (2)		
Top & bottom	1″ wide	× 29½″ (2)		
Border 2—Cradle				
Sides	2½″ wide	× 36½″ (2)		
Top & bottom	2½″ wide	× 33½″ (2)		
Border 1—Crib				
Sides	1″ wide		× 42½″ (2)	
Top & bottom	1″ wide		× 29½″ (2)	
Border 2—Crib				
Sides	4″ wide		× 43½″ (3)	
Top & bottom	3″ wide		× 36½″ (2)	
Border 3—Crib			84 sets	
Border 4—Crib				
Sides	3½″ wide		× 52½″ (3)	
Top & bottom	3½″ wide		× 46½″ (3)	
Border 1—Twin				
Sides	1″ wide			× 91½″ (5)
Top & bottom	1″ wide			× 50½″ (3)
Border 2—Twin				
Sides	3½″ wide			× 92½″ (5)
Top & bottom	2½″ wide			× 56½″ (3)
Border 3—Twin				152 sets
Border 4—Twin				
Sides	4″ wide			× 100½″ (6)
Top & bottom	2½″ wide			× 67½″ (4)
Binding	2½″ × fabric width	4 strips	6 strips	9 strips

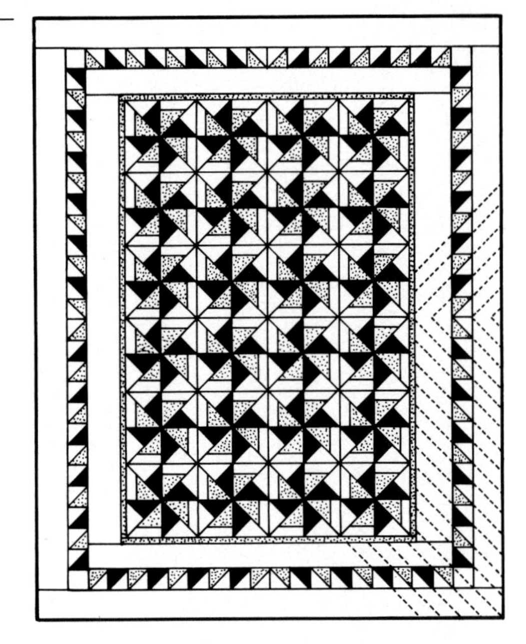

DIRECTIONS: Use ¼″ seams throughout. Refer to *Glossary of Techniques* for specific methods. Follow quilt diagram and add or subtract blocks to obtain desired size.

1. Piece blocks following diagram.
2. Piece blocks together to make rows.
3. Piece rows together following quilt diagram.
4. For borders, follow cutting directions and stitch strips together, if necessary, to make the needed lengths. Stitch first border to quilt sides first then top and bottom. Repeat for second border.
5. Piece muslin and print triangles together for sawtooth border. Piece triangle sets together, observing the direction change at center of each end and side. Add a square (C) to each side of top and bottom borders.
6. Sew pieced border and fourth border to quilt in stairstep fashion starting with sides of quilt.
7. Refer to *Finishing Steps For All Quilts* on page 15. The pinwheel blocks are outline quilted on the small prints and double outline quilted on the muslin background pieces. The border is double-line quilted following the angles of the sawtooth border. See quilt diagram.

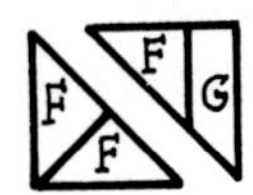

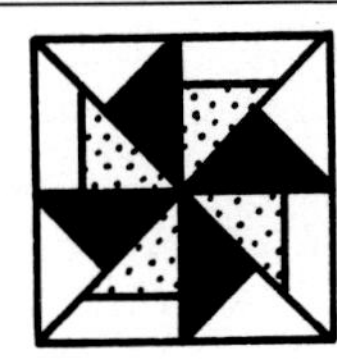

BORDER

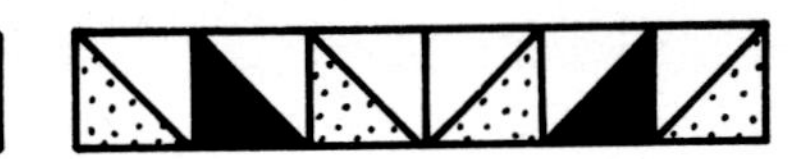

PINWHEELS designed by Nancy Smith and Lynda Milligan, pieced by Sharon Holmes, hand quilted by Gwenn Michal, 1989, 46″ × 58″. This pinwheel crib ensemble offers unlimited possibilities. Using scraps or a purchased combination of fabrics, create a unique nursery by coordinating quilt, bumper pads, sheets, and dust ruffle—a special gift to welcome baby!

POCKET PALS

BLOCK SIZE: 8″
SETTING: Variable star pockets set with alternating plain squares. Stuffed teddies fit into pockets.

	TEMPLATE OR CUT SIZE	CRADLE	CRIB	TWIN
APPROXIMATE FINISHED SIZE		36″ × 36″	36″ × 52″	68″ × 100″
BLOCKS SET		3 × 3	3 × 5	7 × 11
TOTAL NUMBER OF BLOCKS		9 (5 pieced)	15 (8 pieced)	77 (39 pieced)
YARDAGE (42″-45″ width):				
Light print (background and borders)		1¾ yds.	2 yds.	6¼ yds.
Blue prints (stars, pockets, and border triangles)		5 prints–¼ yd. ea.	8 prints–¼ yd. ea.	*8 prints–½ yd. ea.
Brown check (bears)		⅜ yd.	⅝ yd.	*
Red ribbon (¼″)		2½ yds.	4 yds.	½ yd. each bear
Binding		⅜ yd.	½ yd.	¾ yd.
Backing (pieced vertically)		1¼ yds.	1¾ yds.	6⅛ yds.
Batting (48″ width)		1⅛ yds.	1⅝ yds.	6 yds.
Batting (prepackaged)		45″ × 60″	45″ × 60″	90″ × 108″
CUTTING:				
Light Print—				
setting squares	d	4	7	38
small squares (incl. Border 2)	C	24	36	160
triangles (incl. Border 2)	H	96	136	464
Blue prints				
large square	g	1 each of 5	1 each of 8	5 each of 8
triangles (incl. Border 2)	H	20 each of 5	17 each of 8	58 each of 8
pocket	f	2 each of 5	2 each of 8	*
Brown check-bears	(e)-7″ squares	10	16	*
Borders—( )= # of strips to cut				
Border 1				
Sides	2½″ wide	× 24½″ (2)	× 40½″ (2)	× 88½″ (5)
Top & bottom	2½″ wide	× 28½″ (2)	× 28½″ (2)	× 60½″ (3)
Border 2		56 sets	72 sets	152 sets
Border 3				
Sides	2½″ wide	× 32½″ (2)	× 48½″ (3)	× 96½″ (5)
Top & bottom	2½″ wide	× 36½″ (2)	× 36½″ (2)	× 68½″ (4)
Binding	2½″ × fabric width	4 strips	5 strips	9 strips

* We suggest that you make only a few bears and pockets for the twin size quilt. An extra ¼ yd. of one of the blue fabrics will make four pockets and ⅜ yd. of brown check will make several bears. An alternative would be one or two *Pocket Pals* pillows.

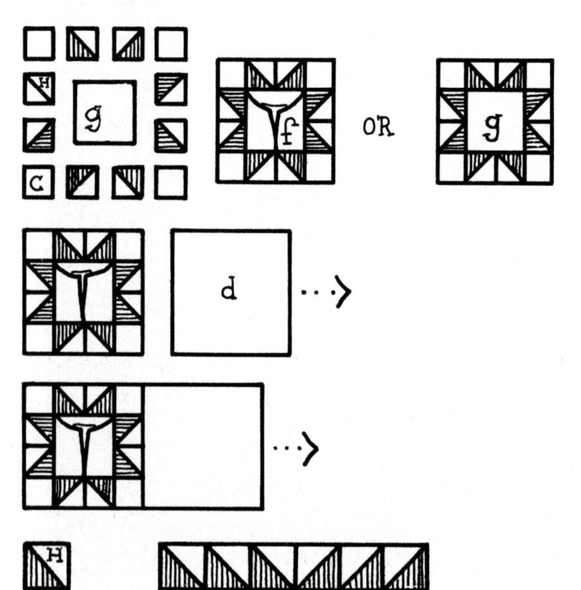

DIRECTIONS: Use ¼″ seams throughout. Refer to *Glossary of Techniques* for specific methods. Follow quilt diagram and add or subtract blocks to obtain desired size.

1. Cut two pieces for each pocket using pocket template (f) for pattern. Place pieces right sides together and stitch along curved edge. Clip curve, turn and press. Lay pocket piece on 4½″ squares (g). Make an inverted pleat in middle along bottom edge as illustrated. Raw edges should match around the square. Press and baste.
2. Piece blocks following diagram.
3. Piece horizontal rows following diagram. Make sure that pockets open to top of quilt.
4. Piece rows together following quilt diagram.
5. For first and third borders, follow cutting directions and stitch strips together, if necessary, to make the needed lengths.
6. Sew first border to quilt sides first then top and bottom.
7. For second border, piece blue triangles and background triangles together. Sew triangle sets together to make lengths needed (see quilt diagram), making sure to alternate direction of triangles at midpoint of each side. Sew second border onto quilt sides first then top and bottom.
8. Sew third border onto quilt sides first then top and bottom.

Continued on page 50.

POCKET PALS by Nancy Smith, hand quilted by Gwenn Michal, 1990, 36″ × 52″. The quilt is not only delightfully appealing, but these "small teddy treasures" become new friends and learning companions for baby.

SAIL AWAY

BLOCK SIZE: 6″
SETTING: Sailboats alternating with nine-patch blocks set straight with sashing and setting squares.

	TEMPLATE OR CUT SIZE	CRADLE	CRIB	TWIN
APPROXIMATE FINISHED SIZE		30″ × 38″	46″ × 54″	70″ × 102″
BLOCKS SET		3 × 4	5 × 6	8 × 12
TOTAL NUMBER OF BLOCKS		12 (6 boats & 6 nine-patch)	30 (15 boats & 15 nine-patch)	96 (48 boats & 48 nine-patch)
YARDAGE (42″-45″ width):				
Light print for background, sashing strips and borders		1½ yds.	2½ yds.	6⅜ yds.
Medium blue print (#1) for sailboats		⅓ yd.	½ yd.	1¼ yds.
Medium blue print (#2) for 9-patches, setting squares and border corners		½ yd.	¾ yd.	1⅞ yds.
Binding		⅜ yd.	½ yd.	¾ yd.
Backing (pieced vertically)		1¼ yds.	3⅜ yds.	6¼ yds.
Batting (48″ width)		1 yd.	1¾ yds.	6 yds.
Batting (prepackaged)		45″ × 60″	72″ × 90″	90″ × 108″
CUTTING:				
Light Print	D	42	105	336
	C	24	60	192
	E	42	105	336
	B	31	71	212
Medium blue (#1)	D	12	30	96
	E	42	105	336
Medium blue (#2)	C	54	121	361
Borders—( )= # of strips to cut				
Sides	2½″ wide	× 34½″ (2)	× 50½″ (3)	× 98½″ (5)
Top & bottom	2½″ wide	× 26½″ (2)	× 42½″ (2)	× 66½″ (4)
Binding	2½″ × fabric width	4 strips	5 strips	9 strips

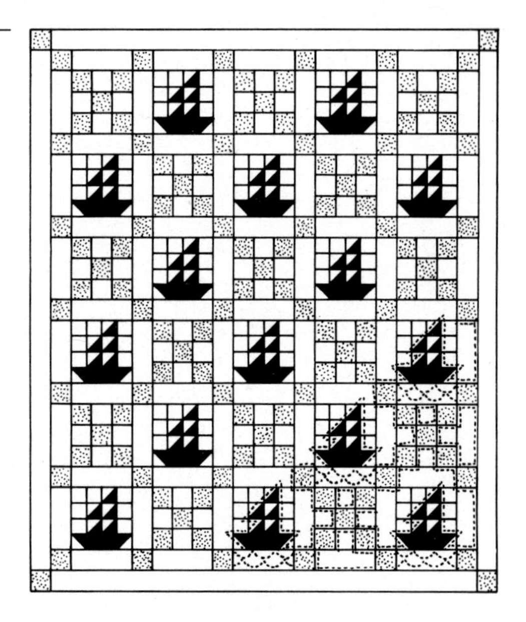

DIRECTIONS: Use ¼″ seams throughout. Refer to *Glossary of Techniques* for specific methods. Follow quilt diagram and add or subtract blocks to obtain desired size.

1. Piece 9-patch blocks following diagram.
2. Piece sailboat blocks following diagram.
3. Piece horizontal rows alternating sashing strips with 9-patch blocks and sailboat blocks. Piece horizontal rows of setting squares and sashing strips.
4. Stitch alternating rows of blocks and pieced sashing.
5. For border, follow cutting directions and stitch strips together, if necessary, to make the needed lengths. Add a square(C) to each end of top and bottom borders.
6. Sew border to quilt sides first then top and bottom.
7. Refer to *Finishing Steps For All Quilts* on page 15. Nine-patch blocks are outline quilted. Sailboats are double outline quilted except for sashing strip at bottom of boat which is quilted in a clamshell design. Quilting design is on page 73. See diagram for placement.

SAIL AWAY by Nancy Smith, hand quilted by Saloma Yoder, 1990, 46″ × 54″. A child's dreams will sail away on waves of imagination when he sleeps under this nautical quilt.

SWEET HEARTS

BLOCK SIZE: 6″
SETTING: Hearts alternating with nine-patch blocks set straight with sashing and setting squares.

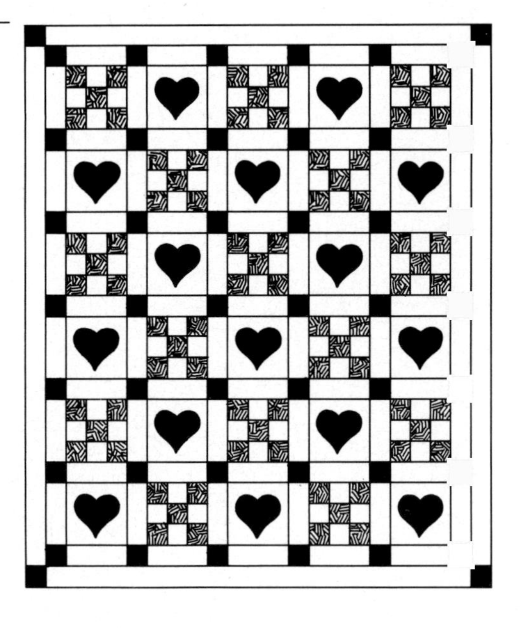

	TEMPLATE OR CUT SIZE	CRADLE	CRIB	TWIN
APPROXIMATE FINISHED SIZE		30″ × 38″	46″ × 54″	70″ × 102″
BLOCKS SET		3 × 4	5 × 6	8 × 12
TOTAL NUMBER OF BLOCKS		12 (6 hearts & 6 nine-patch)	30 (15 hearts & 15 nine-patch)	96 (48 hearts & 48 nine-patch)
YARDAGE (42″-45″ width):				
Background		1¼ yds.	2¼ yds.	5¾ yds.
Dark pink for hearts & setting squares		⅜ yd.	1 yd.	2 yds.
Pink scraps to total		¼ yd.	½ yd.	1¼ yds.
Binding		⅜ yd.	½ yd.	¾ yd.
Backing (pieced vertically)		1¼ yds.	3⅜ yds.	6¼ yds.
Batting (48″ width)		1 yd.	1¾ yds.	6 yds.
Batting (prepackaged)		45″ × 60″	72″ × 90″	90″ × 108″
CUTTING:				
Background				
Applique blocks	A	6	15	48
Nine-patches	C	24	60	192
Sashing strips	B	31	71	212
Dark pink				
Setting squares	C	24	46	121
Hearts	I	6	15	48
Pink scraps	C	30	75	240
Borders—( )= # of strips to cut				
Sides	2½″ wide	× 34½″ (2)	× 50½″ (3)	× 98½″ (5)
Top & bottom	2½″ wide	× 26½″ (2)	× 42½″ (2)	× 66½″ (4)
Binding	2½″ × fabric width	4 strips	5 strips	9 strips

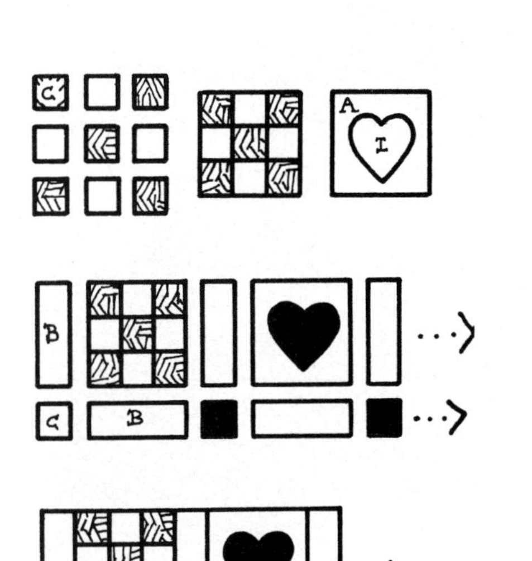

SWEET HEARTS

DIRECTIONS: Use ¼″ seams throughout. Refer to *Glossary of Techniques* for specific methods. Follow quilt diagram and add or subtract blocks to obtain desired size.

1. Piece blocks following diagrams.
2. Applique hearts to centers of 6½″ squares (A).
3. Piece horizontal rows, alternating sashing strips with pieced blocks and appliqued heart blocks. Piece horizontal rows of setting squares and sashing strips.
4. Stitch alternating rows of blocks and pieced sashing.
5. For border, follow cutting directions and stitch strips together, if necessary, to make the needed lengths. Add a square (C) to each end of top and bottom borders.
6. Sew border to quilt sides first then top and bottom.
7. Refer to *Finishing Steps For All Quilts* on page 15. This quilt is machine quilted with straight lines on both sides of pink scrap squares and around appliqued hearts.

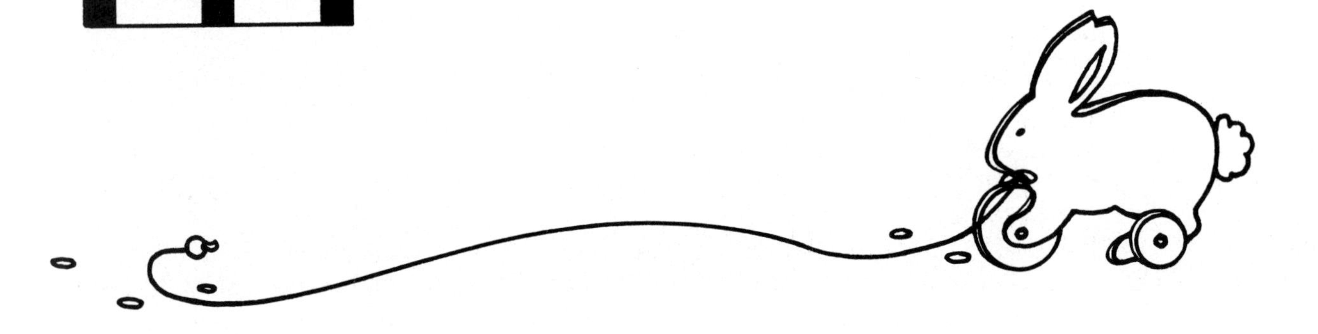

SWEET HEARTS designed by Nancy Smith and Lynda Milligan, pieced and appliqued by Judy Carpenter, machine quilted by Sharon Holmes, 1990, 46″ × 54″. A collection of hearts for baby is always a welcome gift. A simple heart says it all. For *Lullaby* quilt, see page 34.

TIMEWORN TREASURE

BLOCK SIZE: 6″
SETTING: Nine-patch blocks set straight with sashing and setting squares, single border with mitered corners.

	TEMPLATE OR CUT SIZE	CRADLE	CRIB	TWIN
APPROXIMATE FINISHED SIZE		30″ × 38″	46″ × 54″	70″ × 102″
BLOCKS SET		3 × 4	5 × 6	8 × 12
TOTAL NUMBER OF BLOCKS		12	30	96
YARDAGE (42″-45″ width):				
Light scraps to total		½ yd.	1 yd.	2⅝ yds.
Dark scraps to total		⅜ yd.	⅞ yd.	2 yds.
Sashing		⅝ yd.	1⅛ yds.	2¾ yds.
Setting squares—scraps to total		¼ yd.	⅜ yd.	¾ yd.
Border if using stripe		1¼ yds.	1¾ yds.	3⅛ yds.
Border if not stripe		⅜ yd.	⅝ yd.	¾ yd.
Binding		⅜ yd.	½ yd.	¾ yd.
Backing (pieced vertically)		1¼ yds.	3⅜ yds.	6¼ yds.
Batting (48″ width)		1 yd.	1¾ yds.	6 yds.
Batting (prepackaged)		45″ × 60″	72″ × 90″	90″ × 108″
CUTTING:				
Light scraps—nine-patches	C	60	150	480
Dark scraps—nine-patches	C	48	120	384
Sashing	B	31	71	212
Setting squares	C	20	42	117
Border—( )= # of strips to cut				
Sides	2½″ wide	× 42″ (2)	× 58″ (3)	× 76″ (4)
Top & bottom	2½″ wide	× 34″ (2)	× 50″ (3)	× 108″ (6)
Binding	2½″ × fabric width	4 strips	5 strips	9 strips

DIRECTIONS: Use ¼″ seams throughout. Refer to *Glossary of Techniques* for specific methods. Follow quilt diagram and add or subtract blocks to obtain desired size.

1. Piece blocks following diagram.
2. Piece horizontal rows of blocks and sashing strips following diagram. Piece horizontal rows of setting squares and sashing strips.
3. Stitch alternating rows of blocks and pieced sashing.
4. For border, follow cutting directions and stitch strips together, if necessary, to make the needed lengths.
5. Sew border to quilt and miter corners.
6. Refer to *Finishing Steps For All Quilts* on page 15. All pieces are outline quilted by hand.

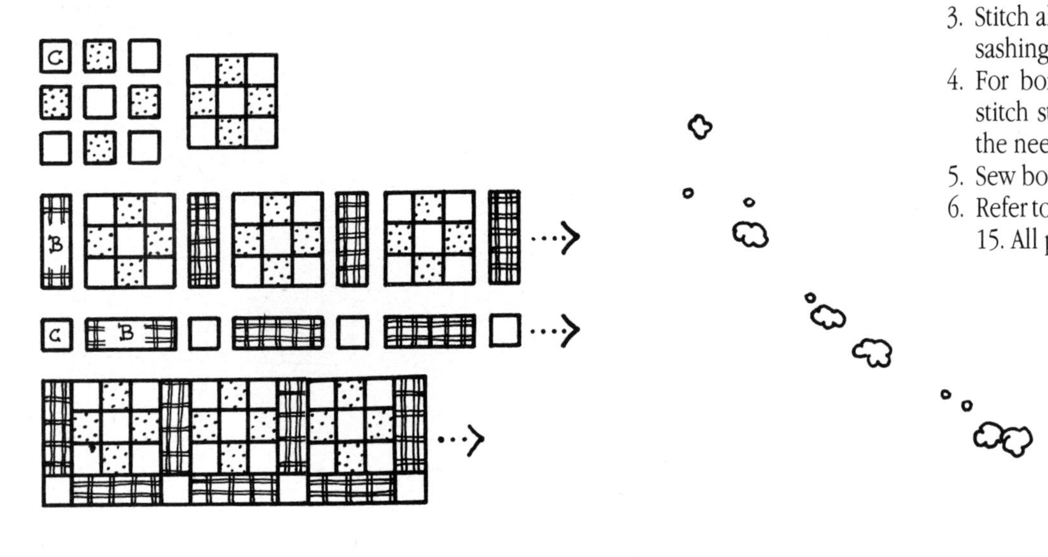

TIMEWORN TREASURE by Nancy Smith, hand quilted by Connie Powell, 1990, 46″ × 54″. This easy nine-patch pattern features homespun fabrics. Accessorized with country decor, it provides a glimpse of long ago.

WATERCOLOR WISHES

BLOCK SIZE: 7½″

SETTING: Log cabin blocks set in a windmill pattern and finished quilt-as-you-go. Pattern pieces are also given for traditional piecing if desired. Follow *Daisy Daisy* piecing directions.

	TEMPLATE OR CUT SIZE	CRADLE	CRIB	TWIN
APPROXIMATE FINISHED SIZE		36″ × 43″	43″ × 58″	73″ × 103″
BLOCKS SET		3 × 4	4 × 6	8 × 12
TOTAL NUMBER OF BLOCKS		12	24	96
YARDAGE (42″-45″ width):				
Center square		⅛ yd.	⅙ yd.	⅜ yd.
1st light green strips		⅛ yd.	¼ yd.	¾ yd.
2nd light green strips		¼ yd.	⅜ yd.	1¼ yds.
3rd light green strips		¼ yd.	½ yd.	1¾ yds.
1st dark lavender strips		¼ yd.	⅜ yd.	1 yd.
2nd dark lavender strips		¼ yd.	½ yd.	1½ yds.
3rd dark lavender strips		⅜ yd.	⅝ yd.	2 yds.
Border 1		½ yd.	⅝ yd.	1 yd.
Border 2		⅝ yd.	⅞ yd.	1¼ yds.
Binding		⅜ yd.	½ yd.	¾ yd.
Backing & batting (quilt-as-you-go/42″-45″ width)		2¼ yds.	3⅝ yds.	10 yds.
Backing (whole top method—pieced vertically)		1½ yds.	3⅝ yds.	6¼ yds.
Batting (whole top method—48″ wide)		1⅛ yds.	1¾ yds.	6 yds.
Batting (whole top method—prepackaged)		45″ × 60″	72″ × 90″	90″ × 108″
CUTTING:				
For quilt-as-you-go, cut fabric into strips 1½″ wide × fabric width. For whole-top method, use templates in 2nd column.				
Center square	D	12	24	96
1st light (green)	O	12	24	96
	P	12	24	96
1st dark (lavender)	P	12	24	96
	Q	12	24	96
2nd light (green)	Q	12	24	96
	R	12	24	96
2nd dark (lavender)	R	12	24	96
	S	12	24	96
3rd light (green)	S	12	24	96
	T	12	24	96
3rd dark (lavender)	T	12	24	96
	U	12	24	96
Borders—( )= # of strips to cut				
Border 1				
Sides	3″ wide	× 30½″ (2)	× 45½″ (3)	× 90½″ (5)
Top & bottom	3″ wide	× 28″ (2)	× 35½″ (2)	× 65½″ (4)
Border 2				
Sides	4½″ wide	× 35½″ (2)	× 50½″ (3)	× 95½″ (5)
Top & bottom	4½″ wide	× 36″ (2)	× 43½″ (3)	× 73½″ (4)
Backing & batting for quilt-as-you-go				
Squares	10″ sq.	12	24	96
Border				
Sides	10″ wide	× 30½″ (2)	× 45½″ (2)	× 90½″ (2)
Top & bottom	10″ wide	× 43″ (2)	× 50½″ (2)	× 80½″ (2)
Binding	2½″ × fabric width	4 strips	5 strips	9 strips

DIRECTIONS: Use ¼″ seams throughout. Refer to *Glossary of Techniques* for specific methods. Follow quilt diagram and add or subtract blocks to obtain desired size. This quilt was assembled with the quilt-as-you-go method.

1. Cut borders and 10″ squares from backing and batting. See entry above binding on cutting chart. Cut borders lengthwise before cutting squares.
2. Mark from corner to corner across batting squares, making sure that center lines are at right angles. Lay square on backing.
3. Lay center square on batting; line up corners with marked lines.
4. Lay first light strip face down on center square. Stitch along right edge with ¼″ seam allowance. Fold strip back on itself and cut even with center square. Open out and finger press.
5. Turn block ¼ turn counterclockwise. Lay same light strip face down on center square and previous strip. Stitch. Fold back and cut even. Open out strip and finger press.
6. Again, turn block ¼ turn counterclockwise. Lay first dark strip face down on center block and previous strip. Stitch. Fold back and cut even. Open out strip and finger press.

Continued on page 50.

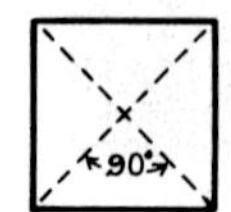

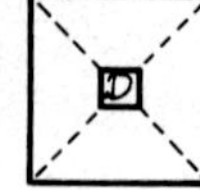

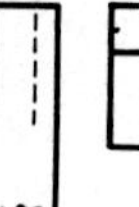
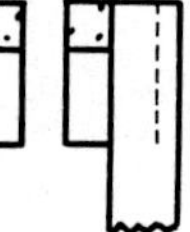
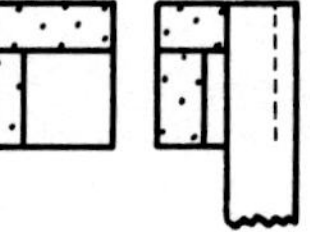
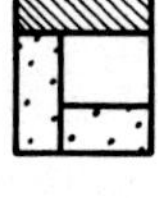
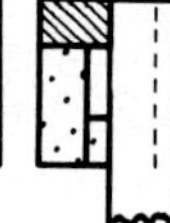
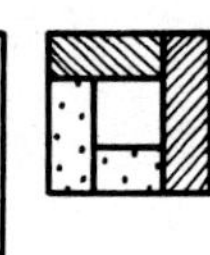

WATERCOLOR WISHES by Lynda Milligan, 1990, 43″ × 58″. Inspired by a waterfall of cool running water, this log cabin quilt is quickly assembled with the quilt-as-you go method.

WOVEN RIBBONS

BLOCK SIZE: 3″
SETTING: Blocks set straight, alternating direction of color families. Great for a signature memory quilt.

	TEMPLATE OR CUT SIZE	CRADLE	CRIB	TWIN
APPROXIMATE FINISHED SIZE		32″ × 44″	44″ × 56″	68″ × 104″
BLOCKS SET		8 × 12	12 × 16	20 × 32
TOTAL NUMBER OF BLOCKS		96	192	640
YARDAGE (42″-45″ width):				
Pink print #1		⅓ yd.	½ yd.	1½ yds.
Pink print #2		⅓ yd.	½ yd.	1½ yds.
Green print #1		⅓ yd.	½ yd.	1½ yds.
Green print #2		⅓ yd.	½ yd.	1½ yds.
Muslin		½ yd.	1 yd.	2¾ yds.
Border 1		⅓ yd.	⅜ yd.	½ yd.
Border 2		⅝ yd.	¾ yd.	1⅛ yds.
Binding		⅜ yd.	½ yd.	¾ yd.
Backing (pieced vertically)		1½ yds.	3⅝ yds.	6¼ yds.
Batting (48″ width)		1 yd.	1¾ yds.	6 yds.
Batting (prepackaged)		45″ × 60″	72″ × 90″	90″ × 108″
CUTTING:				
Pink print #1	Y	48	96	320
Pink print #2	Y	48	96	320
Green print #1	Y	48	96	320
Green print #2	Y	48	96	320
Muslin	Y	96	192	640
Borders—( )= # of strips to cut				
Border 1				
Sides	1½″ wide	× 48″ (3)	× 60″ (3)	× 108″ (6)
Top & bottom	1½″ wide	× 36″ (2)	× 48″ (3)	× 72″ (4)
Border 2				
Sides	3½″ wide	× 48″ (3)	× 60″ (3)	× 108″ (6)
Top & bottom	3½″ wide	× 36″ (2)	× 48″ (3)	× 72″ (4)
Binding	2½″ × fabric width	4 strips	5 strips	9 strips

DIRECTIONS: Use ¼″ seams throughout. Refer to *Glossary of Techniques* for specific methods. Follow quilt diagram and add or subtract blocks to obtain desired size.

1. Piece blocks following diagram. Piece half the blocks with muslin and the two pinks and the other half of the blocks with muslin and the two greens.
2. Piece horizontal rows alternating color and direction of blocks.
3. Piece rows together following quilt diagram.
4. For borders, follow cutting directions and stitch strips together, if necessary, to make the needed lengths.
5. Sew borders to quilt and miter corners.
6. Refer to *Finishing Steps For All Quilts* on page 15. Machine quilt in the ditch between all blocks and borders.

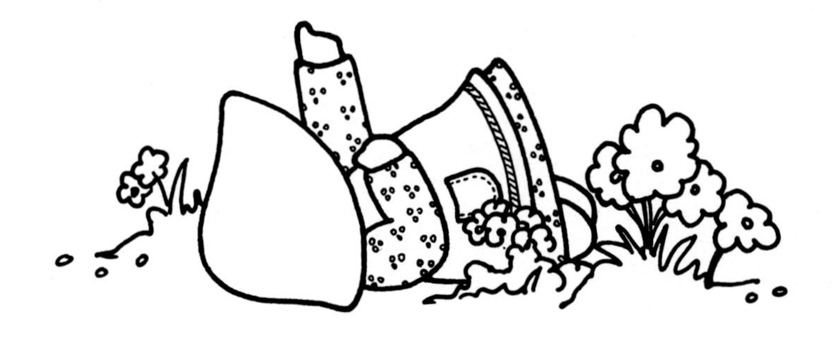

WOVEN RIBBONS by Lynda Milligan, machine quilted by Sharon Holmes, 1990, 44″ × 56″. Inspired by woven ribbon pillows of the past, this very lovely pattern makes a wonderful autograph quilt.

HEART OF MY HEART
Continued from page 28.

11. For borders, follow cutting directions and stitch strips together, if necessary, to make the needed lengths. Sew borders to quilt in stairstep fashion starting with top and bottom of quilt.
12. Refer to *Finishing Steps For All Quilts* on page 15. The muslin squares and fans are outline quilted. A heart is quilted in the corner of each muslin square and triangle. Quilting design is on page 74. See quilt diagram for placement.

POCKET PALS
Continued from page 38.

9. Refer to *Finishing Steps For All Quilts* on page 15. Quilting design is on page 74. See quilt diagram for placement.

To Make Teddies:

1. Make a template of teddy pattern.
2. Layer two 7″ squares of teddy fabric with right sides together. Lay template on wrong side of fabric and draw around it. Do not cut!
3. Stitch on drawn line or slightly inside, leaving open between "x's".
4. Cut out, leaving a scant ¼″ seam allowance. Clip curves and inside points. Turn.
5. Stuff teddy, leaving ears unstuffed. Stitch opening closed. Tack base of each ear closed by sewing a few small stitches.
6. Use black marker to make eyes; use red marker for nose and mouth; blush cheeks with red pencil.
7. Tie ribbon bow around neck.

WATERCOLOR WISHES
Continued from page 46.

7. Turn block ¼ turn counterclockwise. Lay same dark strip face down and continue as above. Now there is one row on the block—two light strips and two dark strips. Continue adding strips, two of second light, two of second dark, two of third light and two of third dark, making sure that batting and backing squares remain smooth and unpuckered. On the last row, begin and end stitching of strips ¼″ from outside edge. Press well.
8. Trim backing and batting slightly larger than pieced blocks.
9. Arrange blocks in chosen pattern.
10. Pin rows together through batting and pieced block only. Be sure not to catch backing. Stitch.
11. Press seams from right side.
12. Flip quilt over. Working from wrong side, lap one seam allowance over another. Turn in ¼″ and applique in place making sure that stitching does not show on quilt front.
13. For borders, follow cutting directions and stitch strips together, if necessary, to make the needed lengths. Sew sides of first border on first-layer in the following order with raw edges even: batting, border backing (right side up), quilt top (right side up) and first border (right side down). Stitch with ¼″ seam. Open out and press well. Trim ends of border backing and batting even with ends of quilt, if necessary. Attach batting, border backing and first border to the top and bottom of quilt in the same sequence. Open out and press well. Trim ends, if necessary. Lay sides of second border with raw edges even with first border. Stitch through backing and batting with ¼″ seam. Take care to keep backing smooth. Trim ends. Finish top and bottom of second border with same method. Trim ends. Press well. Trim batting and backing even with top.
14. Bind quilt referring to *Glossary of Techniques* for directions.

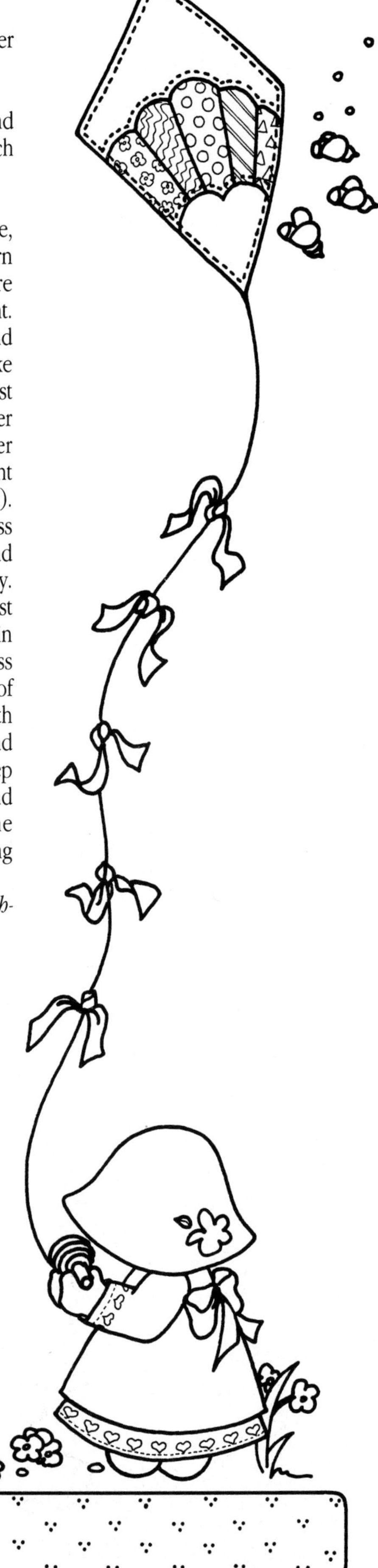

ACCESSORIES

CRIB ACCESSORIES

Use ¼″ seam allowance throughout unless otherwise noted.

CRIB SHEET

Pictured on page 37.
To fit a standard crib mattress (27″ × 52″)

Yardage and Supplies:

Fabric (42″-45″)—2 yds.
½″ wide single-fold bias tape—4½ yds. (optional)
¼″ elastic—1 yd.
Matching thread

To Make Crib Sheet:

1. Cut a rectangle from fabric 43″ × 68″.
2. Cut out an 8″ square from each corner. See illustration.
3. With right sides together, pin and stitch edge "b" to edge "a" of each corner. Sew with a ¼″ seam allowance.
4. Fold bias tape in half lengthwise and press. Slip folded edge over raw edge of sheet and pin. Machine stitch bias tape using a straight stitch or a small zig-zag. Optional hem: To eliminate bias tape, press under ¼″ then ¼″ again to make hem. Stitch.
5. Using a 9″ length of elastic, pin the center of the elastic to the wrong side of each sheet corner with the edge of the elastic about ⅛″ from bias tape or hemmed edge. Machine stitch from this center point along elastic with a zig-zag stitch, stretching elastic as tight as possible. Start from center and stitch to other end of elastic. Repeat for other end of elastic. Repeat for other three corners.

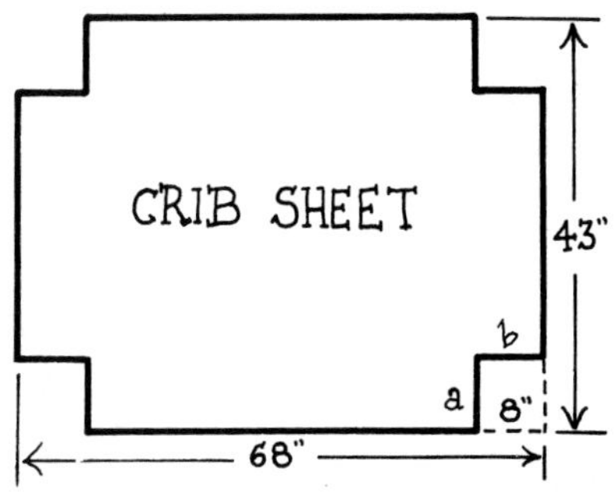

BUMPER PADS

Pictured on page 37.
Six units with finished measurements of approximately 10″ × 26″ each

Yardage for Basic Bumpers:

Foam 1″ thick—enough to cut six pieces 8½″ × 24½″
Batting—2¼ yds. of 48″ wide, 6 oz. batting
Cording—4⅞ yds. of size #150
Fabric (42″-45″)—¾ yd. for one bumper the same on both sides *or* 1⅝ yds. each of two colors for six bumpers using different colors on each side (2 yds. if fabric is directional on the lengthwise grain) *or* 3¼ yds. for six bumpers using same color on both sides (4 yds. if fabric is directional on the lengthwise grain)
Fabric for cording—⅜ yd.
Matching thread

Cutting for Basic Bumpers:

6 pieces of foam—8½″ × 24½″
6 pieces of batting—19″ × 24½″
6 pieces of cording—28″ long
6 pieces of fabric—1½″ × 28″ for cording
6 pieces of fabric—11½″ × 27″ for bumper pad fronts
6 pieces of fabric—11½″ × 27″ for bumper pad facings
24 pieces of fabric—1½″ × 14″ for ties

To Make Basic Bumpers:

1. Lay cording along the center of wrong side of 1½″ × 28″ pieces of fabric. Fold fabric over cording, aligning the raw edges. Using a zipper foot and a medium stitch length, baste with matching thread. Sew close to cord but not too close. Repeat for remaining five cording pieces.
2. With right sides together and raw edges even, machine baste each cording piece to one long edge of each of the bumper pad fronts. Sew on the same stitching line as before.
3. Press long edges of tie pieces in ¼″. Fold in half lengthwise and sew, turning in seam allowance on one short end. Repeat for other 23 ties. Pin ties, with raw edges even, to the short ends of the six bumper pad fronts. Pin them 1″ from top edges and 1½″ from bottom edges. Pin loose ends of ties down so they do not get caught while sewing.
4. Pin the facing piece onto each bumper pad. Stitch, starting at "X" and ending at "Y". Stitch as close to cording as possible. Leave bottom edge open for stuffing. Trim corners, turn right sides out, and press. Wrap batting pieces around foam pieces and stuff into bumper pads with folded edges of batting toward top edges of bumpers. Turn one seam allowance over the other and whipstitch closed by hand.

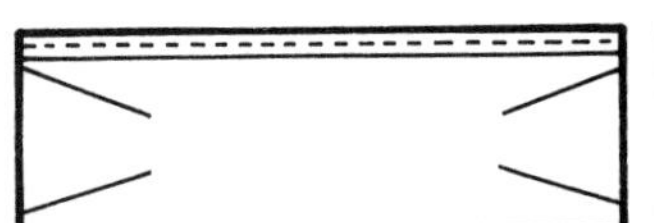

PINWHEELS BUMPER PAD

Pictured on page 37.

Yardage for *One* Pieced Pinwheels Bumper:

For blocks, use scraps from the *Pinwheels* quilt, or purchase ¼ yd. of a multi-colored floral, ⅛ yd. each of three small prints, and ¼ yd. muslin. (Purchase 3¼ yds. main color to complete the *Pinwheels* bumper and the other 5 plain bumpers in the set. If fabric is directional on the lengthwise grain, purchase 4 yds.)

Cutting for *One* Pieced Pinwheels Bumper:

Cut of multi-colored floral:
- Two pieces 1″ × 21½″ (A)
- Two pieces 1″ × 8½″ (B)

Cut of main color:
- Two pieces 2″ × 22½″ (C)
- Two pieces 3″ × 11½″ (D)

See *Basic Bumpers* above for cutting fabric for other 5 plain bumpers as well as facings, foam, batting, cording and ties for all 6 bumpers.

To Make Pinwheels Bumper:

1. Piece three pinwheel blocks referring to *Pinwheels* quilt on page 36. Stitch blocks to one another in a row.
2. Stitch "A" to top and bottom of row of 3 blocks. Stitch "B" to ends of row of blocks.
3. Stitch "C" to top and bottom and "D" to ends. Press.
4. Complete bumper set referring to directions for *Basic Bumpers* above.

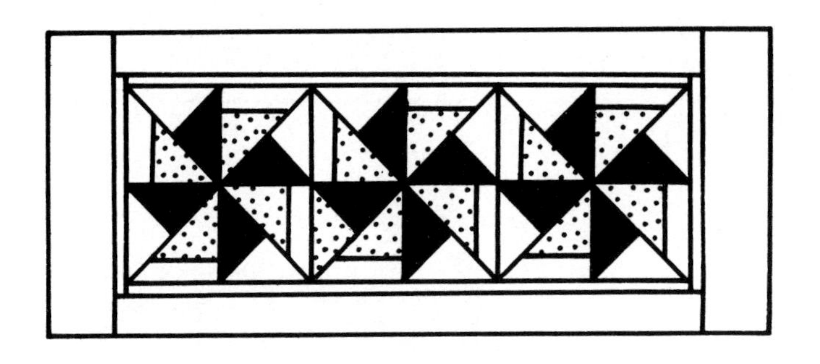

DUST RUFFLE WITH PIECED INSET

Pictured on page 37.

Yardage (42″-45″ wide fabric):

Muslin—4¾ yds.
Scraps to total ½ yd.

To Make Dust Ruffle With Pieced Inset:

1. Cut muslin pieces following measurements given in cutting layout.
2. Using triangle template "H", cut out 156 muslin and 156 scrap triangles. Piece together into squares as illustrated. Stitch squares into two rows of 26 for ends and two rows of 52 for sides. Press.

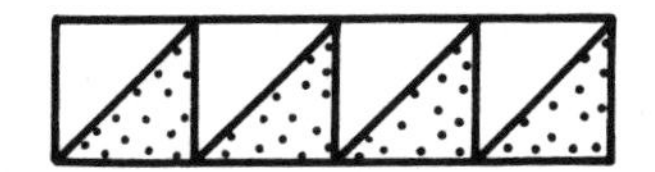

3. Stitch rows of squares to 8½″ wide muslin strips with muslin triangles next to strip. Be careful not to stitch off points of triangles. Press seam toward muslin strip.
4. Press 5″ strips in half lengthwise, right side out. Lay rows of squares right side down onto pressed strip, raw edges even. Stitch with ¼″ seam, being careful not to stitch off points of triangles. Press seam toward muslin strip.

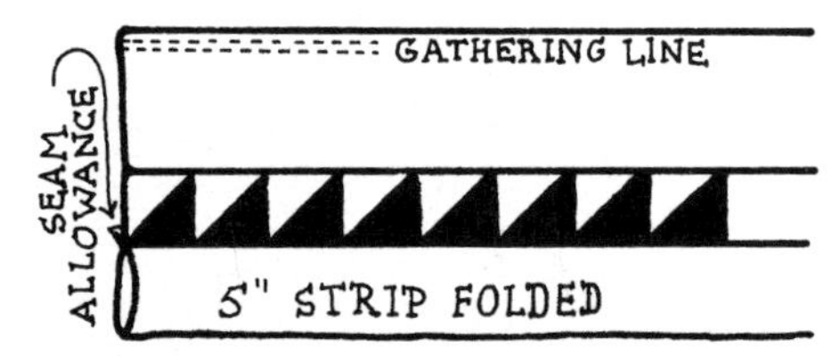

5. Place facing strips onto short ends of ruffle, right sides together and with ½″ extending at bottom edge. Stitch in ¼″ seam. Fold up extended edge; turn facing to wrong side and press; tuck in ¼″ on facing to hide raw edges; topstitch in place.
6. Run two rows of gathering on top edge of 8½″ strip, ⅛″ apart and ½″ from raw edge.
7. Attach ruffles to ends of center panel first: Pull up gathering evenly to 26″. Pin to panel, right sides together, leaving ½″ of center panel free at either end. Stitch with ½″ seam allowance.
8. For side ruffles, pull up gathering evenly to 51″. Pin to panel right sides together, folding under the ½″ extension of center panel seam allowance at each end. Stitch with ½″ seam allowance. Press seams toward center panel. Optional: Topstitch seam to center panel.

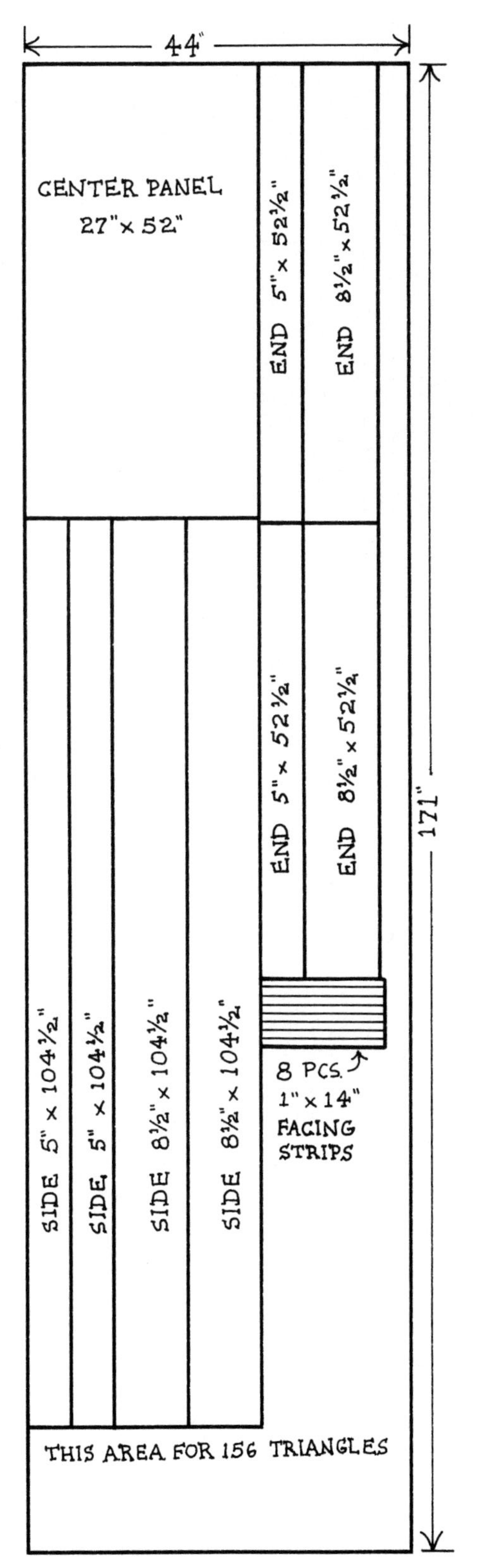

PIECED
DUST RUFFLE

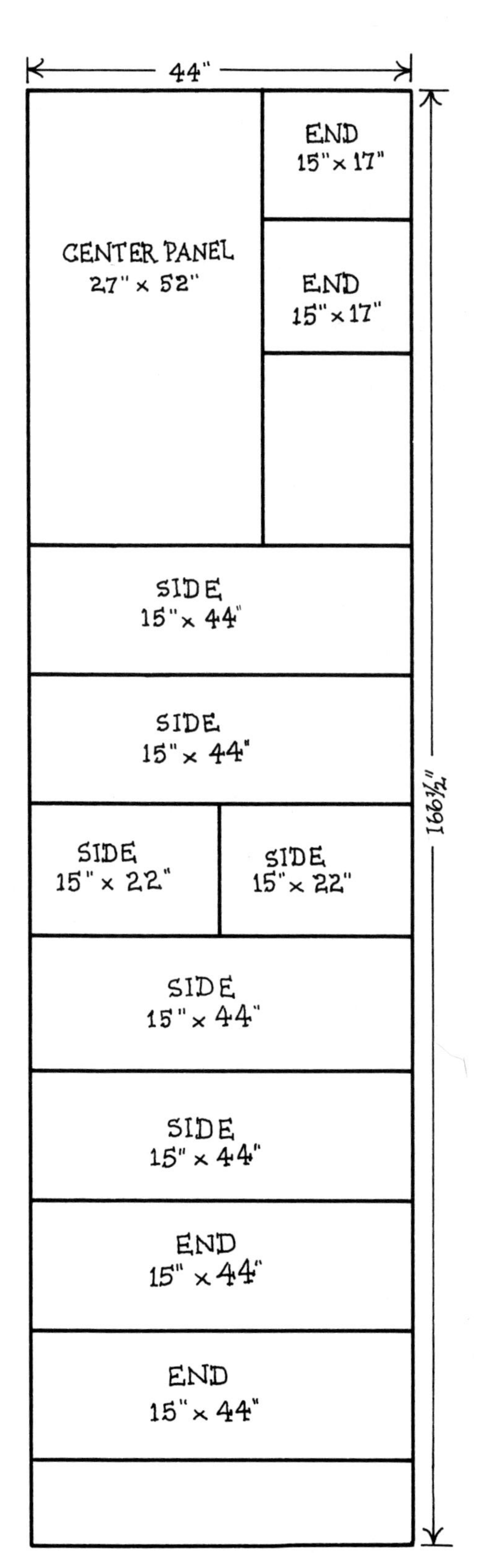

PLAIN
DUST RUFFLE

SIDE = 44"+44"+22"
END = 44"+17"

DUST RUFFLE
Yardage (42″-45″ wide fabric):
4⅝ yds.

To Make Dust Ruffle:
1. Cut fabric pieces following measurements given in cutting layout on page 53.
2. Press up ¼″ on one long edge of each ruffle section. Press up 2¼″ hem and stitch.
3. Press ¼″ of each short edge of each ruffle section to wrong side. Press over ¼″ again. Stitch to make finished edges.
4. Run two rows of gathering on top edge of each ruffle section, ⅛″ apart and ½″ from raw edge.
5. See *Dust Ruffle With Pieced Inset,* steps 7 and 8 above, for finishing.

DECORATIONS

FABRIC PINWHEEL
Pictured on page 54.
Warning: This is *not* a child's toy. Use it for decoration only.
Yardage and Supplies:
Fabric—two 9″ squares
Pellon® Craft-Bond™—two 9″ squares
Pellon® Wonder-Under™—one 9″ square
One new eraser from a pencil
One wooden dowel—approximately ⅜″ in diameter
One very heavy sewing pin **or** very fine nail
One large sequin
One small bead
Glue gun or tacky glue
Wire cutters

To Make Pinwheel:
1. Bond wrong sides of fabric squares with Craft-Bond™. Bond the 2 prepared fabric squares, wrong sides together, with Wonder-Under™ following manufacturer's directions. Cut out a perfect 8″ square from prepared fabric.
2. With a pencil, draw lines on 8″ square from corner to corner forming an "X". Cut along these lines from each corner to 3½″ from corner as illustrated.
3. Bring every other corner to center as illustrated. Pass pin or nail through sequin, through 4 front pinwheel corners, through pencil eraser, through back of pinwheel, and through dowel. Glue bead over extending pin or nail and clip off excess pin or nail shaft.

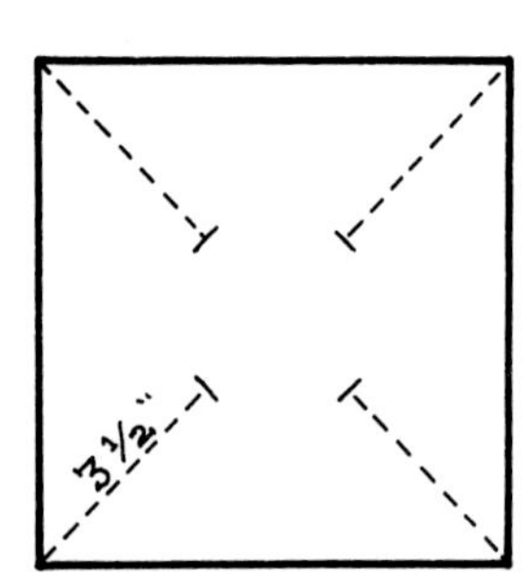

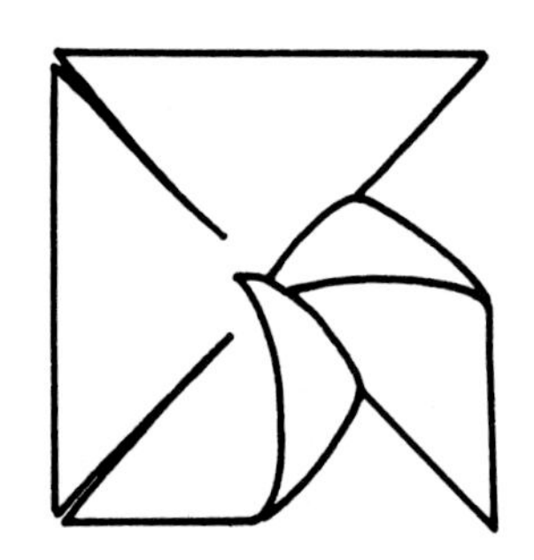

HANGING HEARTS (5″ hearts)
Pictured on page 23.
Yardage and Supplies:
Scraps of fabric at least 6″ square
Small amount of stuffing
Matching thread
⅜″ ribbon—2 yds. each of pink and blue
Glue gun or tacky glue (optional)

To Make Hanging Hearts:
1. Make two 5″ hearts referring to step 1 of *Stars and Hearts Mobile* on page 54.
2. Make two ribbon clusters and attach one to the top of each heart.
3. Cut two pieces of ribbon, one pink and one blue, 22″ long. Lay the ribbons together and treat them as one. Glue or sew one end of ribbon to top of each heart under ribbon cluster, tucking under raw ends of ribbons. Hang over doorknob or end of crib.

STARS AND HEARTS MOBILE (8″ circle)
Pictured on pages 37 and 55.
Yardage and Supplies:
Fabric (42″-45″):
⅛ yd. to cover ring
Scraps of various soft-colored calicos at least 7″ square for large star and 3½″ for small stars and hearts
One plastic circle 9″ in diameter that has an opening or split. (We used an expandable plastic apron clip by Dritz® which is available from most fabric stores in the notions department.)
Matching thread
Template plastic
Small amounts of stuffing
1/16″ ribbon—1 yd. each of pink, green, blue and yellow
¼″ ribbon—3 yds. pink and 1 yd. blue
Glue gun and glue sticks

To Make Mobile:
1. Make eight small hearts (2¼″), eight small stars (2¼″) and two large stars (5½″): Make a template of desired pattern. Place

template on wrong side of one piece of fabric and draw around it. DO NOT CUT OUT! Place the right side of this piece of fabric to the right side of a corresponding size piece of fabric (not necessarily the same print). Stitch on marked line around shape, leaving an opening to turn. Cut out shape ⅛″ to ¼″ from stitching. Trim points, clip curves, and clip inside points to stitching. Turn. Stuff firmly and whipstitch opening closed.

2. To make a casing for plastic circle, cut one strip of fabric 2″ wide by width of fabric. Fold in half lengthwise, right sides facing, and stitch using ¼″ seam allowance. Turn right side out and press. Slide plastic ring through casing. Overlap ends of ring and fabric, tucking in raw edges, and glue in place.
3. Visually divide circle into eight equal parts. Alternate ribbon color and stars and hearts around circle. Cut four 8″ pieces of 1/16″ ribbon for stars and four 12″ pieces of 1/16″ ribbon for hearts. Tie alternate lengths of short and long ribbon around circle at all eight divisions. Glue ribbons to hearts and stars. Tie small bows of matching ribbon and glue them over all glued ribbon ends.
4. Cut four 22″ pieces of pink ¼″ ribbon. Visually divide ring into four equal parts and tie ribbons at these divisions.
5. Pull all four ribbons up and tie together in a knot. Glue knot between the two large stars, allowing ribbons to extend out the top. Trim if necessary.
6. Using the blue ¼″ ribbon, tie a bow and glue it to very tip of star. Use long end of ribbon as a hanger for the mobile.

STRING OF BLOCKS (34″ long)

Pictured on page 37.

Yardage and Supplies:

Small scraps of soft-colored calicos
Small amount of stuffing
Matching thread
⅜″ white ribbon—2½ yds.
Glue gun or tacky glue (optional)

To Make String of Blocks:

1. Make fourteen 1½″ blocks according to block directions on page 57.
2. Tack blocks corner to corner, making a string of 14 blocks.
3. Make a ribbon cluster as shown and glue or tack to each end of string. Attach a long ribbon to each end for tying to crib.

PILLOWS

BASIC PILLOW CONSTRUCTION

Pillow Form

Pillow forms may be purchased from fabric and craft stores, or it is very easy to make them. A word of caution about ready-made forms: They are often larger than the size given on the package. If a specific size is needed, be sure to measure the form with a tape measure before purchasing it. To ensure a smooth pillow, a pillow form about 1″ larger than the desired finished pillow size is needed (i.e., if a 15″ pillow is desired, buy or make a 16″ form). To make a form, cut two squares of muslin or needlepunch the size of the pillow top **plus** 1″. Sew around the four sides of the muslin or needlepunch pieces with a ¼″ seam allowance, leaving an opening on one side. Clip corners, turn and stuff to desired firmness. Hand or machine stitch opening closed. Insert form into pillow top and add a little extra stuffing to pillow corners if necessary.

Envelope Back for Pillow

Measure pillow top. Using that measurement, cut one piece of fabric for front and two pieces for back. Lay fabric for top of pillow right side up. Place one backing piece wrong side up on top of pillow front. Fold up from bottom edge until about one-third of pillow top is showing. Place second square face down onto other square and fold down from top edge until overlap is approximately equal. Pin well and stitch around entire outside edge. Clip corners, turn, press.

Cording for Pillow

Cut a piece of size #150 cording equal to the total distance around pillow edge. Cut a bias strip of fabric 1½″ wide by the length of the cording. Lay cording along center of fabric strip on wrong side. Fold fabric over cording, aligning the raw edges. Using a zipper foot, stitch with matching thread using a long stitch length. Sew close to the cord but not too close since it will be sewn to pillow between this stitching and the cording. Beginning at middle of one side, lay cording on right side of pillow top, all raw edges even. Using a zipper foot and a long stitch length, stitch covered cording to pillow. Stop 1½″ before each corner; make several diagonal cuts into cording seam allowance almost to stitching. Gently curve cording around corners. At the end, cross ends over each other and finish stitching over cording. Cording can be pulled out and trimmed back to make this crossover lay flat.

Ruffle for Pillow

Measure total distance around pillow edge. Double that measurement. Cut strips that length by double the desired width plus ½″ for seam allowance (i.e., for a 12″ square pillow with a 2″ doubled ruffle, cut fabric 48″ × 2 = 96″ long by 2 × 2″ + ½″ = 4½″ wide). Seam shorter pieces together if necessary to make required length. Seam ends of strip together to make one continuous fabric loop. Fold loop in half lengthwise, with right side out, and press. Run two rows of gathering stitches along raw edge inside the ¼″ seam allowance. Fold ruffle into quarters and mark quarter points. With right sides together and raw edges even, pin ruffle to pillow top, matching corners to quarter markings. Pull up gathers evenly, allowing a little extra fullness at corners. Baste in place.

PLAIN PILLOW AND PLAIN PILLOW WITH CORDING (9″)

Pictured on pages 23, 33 and 47.

Yardage and Supplies:

Fabric (42″-45″)—⅜ yd.
Matching thread
Polyester stuffing
Cording—size #150—1⅛ yds. (optional)
Fabric to cover cording—⅓ yd. (optional)

To Make Pillow:

1. Cut two pieces of fabric 9½″ × 9½″ for top and back. Skip to step 3 if not making cording.
2. Prepare bias strip of fabric to cover cording 1½″ × 38″. Follow *Cording For Pillow* directions under *Basic Pillow Construction* above.
3. With right sides of top and back together, stitch around outer edge of pillow. Leave an opening along one side. Trim corners, turn and stuff firmly. Whipstitch opening closed.

RUFFLED PILLOW AND RUFFLED PILLOW WITH STUFFED HEARTS (9″)

Pictured on pages 23, 33 and 55.

Yardage and Supplies:

Fabric (42″-45″)—½ yd.
Matching thread
Polyester stuffing
1/16″ to ¼″ ribbon—2½ yds. (optional)
Scraps of various soft-colored calicos at least 3½″ square for hearts (optional)
Button (optional)

To Make Pillow:

1. Cut two pieces of fabric 9½″ × 9½″ for top and back. Prepare one ruffle 4½″ × 72″.
2. Stitch 4½″ ends of ruffle together. Follow directions for making ruffle in *Ruffle For Pillow* directions under *Basic Pillow Construction* above.
3. With right sides of top and back together, stitch around outer edge of pillow, sewing ruffle in place. Leave an opening along one side. Trim corners, turn and stuff firmly. Whipstitch opening closed.
4. If desired, make hearts referring to directions with *Stars and Hearts Mobile* on page 55. Make ribbon cluster and tack stuffed heart at center. Tack ribbon cluster to pillow. Or: Tack hearts to knots tied near ribbon ends and then tack hearts and ribbon cluster to pillow. Add decorative button if desired.

LOLLIPOPS AND LEMONDROPS PILLOW (10″)

Pictured on pages 35, 43 and 55.

Yardage and Supplies:

Fabric A (sashing strips)—⅛ yd.
Fabric B (back, ruffle, setting squares)—½ yd.
Fabric C (center square)—¼ yd.
Matching thread
Polyester stuffing

To Make Pillow:

1. Piece pillow top referring to *Lollipops and Lemondrops* quilt on page 32. The pillow top is one block surrounded by sashing and setting squares.
2. Cut one back 10½″ square. Prepare one ruffle piece 4½″ × 80″.
3. Finish referring to steps 2 and 3 of *Ruffled Pillow* above.

LULLABY PILLOW (10″)

Pictured on pages 35, 43 and 55.

Yardage and Supplies:

Fabric A (pinwheel)—⅛ yd.
Fabric B (sashing strips)—⅛ yd.
Fabric C (pinwheel background, setting squares)—1/6 yd.
Fabric D (pinwheel, ruffle, back)—¾ yd.
Matching thread
Polyester stuffing

To Make Pillow:

1. Piece pillow top referring to *Lullaby* quilt on page 34. Follow directions for making one block surrounded by sashing and setting squares.
2. Cut one pillow back 10½″ square. Prepare one ruffle 6½″ × 80″. Stitch the 6½″ ends of the ruffle together.
3. Finish referring to steps 2 and 3 of *Ruffled Pillow* above.

BABY TEARS PILLOW (11½″)

Pictured on page 55.

Yardage and Supplies:

Fabric A (patchwork, corner squares, backing)—½ yd.
Fabric B (border)—⅛ yd.
Scraps—8 coordinated 2″ squares
Matching thread
Polyester stuffing

To Make Pillow:

1. Piece pillow top referring to *Baby Tears* quilt on page 18. Make four 4-patch units of fabric A and scraps and set together with fabric A using half and quarter triangles for the outside edges.
2. Cut four 2″ squares of fabric A for outer corner. Cut four pieces 2″ × 9″ from fabric B.
3. Assemble pillow top as follows: Cut one pillow back 12″ square. With right sides together, stitch top and back around entire outer edge, leaving an opening along one side. Trim corners, turn and stuff firmly. Whipstitch opening closed.

BABY TEARS PILLOW WITH RUFFLE (14¾″)

Pictured on page 55.

Yardage and Supplies:

Muslin (back, ruffle, patchwork)—1 yd.
Scraps—18 coordinated 2″ squares
Matching thread
Polyester stuffing

To Make Pillow:

1. Piece pillow referring to *Baby Tears* quilt on page 18. Make nine 4-patch units of muslin and scraps and set together with muslin using half and quarter triangles for the outside edges.
2. Cut two borders 1½″ × 13¼″ and two borders 1½″ × 15¼″.
3. Stitch 1½″ × 13¼″ strips to opposite sides. Stitch other two strips to remaining sides.
4. Prepare ruffle strip 5½″ × 112″.
5. Cut one pillow back 15¼″ square. Stitch the 5½″ ends of the ruffle together.
6. Finish pillow by referring to steps 2 and 3 of *Ruffled Pillow* above.

SQUARE-KNOT PILLOW (any size)

Pictured on page 33.

A wonderfully fun and fast pillow for any room in the house!

Yardage and Supplies:

Square pillow form, purchased or self-made (see *Pillow Form* under *Basic Pillow Construction* above)
Square of fabric equal to 2½ times the size of pillow form (i.e., 12″ pillow form would need a square of fabric 2½ × 12″ or 30″)
One safety pin

To Make Pillow:

1. Lay fabric square right side down. Place pillow form on square, having corners of form point toward centers of sides of fabric square.
2. Fold "A" corners in to meet pillow form.
3. Bring folded edges up to overlap center of pillow form. Pull firmly and pin in place.
4. Pull up "B" corners to center of pillow, tucking in all raw edges, and tie a square knot in center of pillow. Tuck raw ends of "B" corners under the knot.

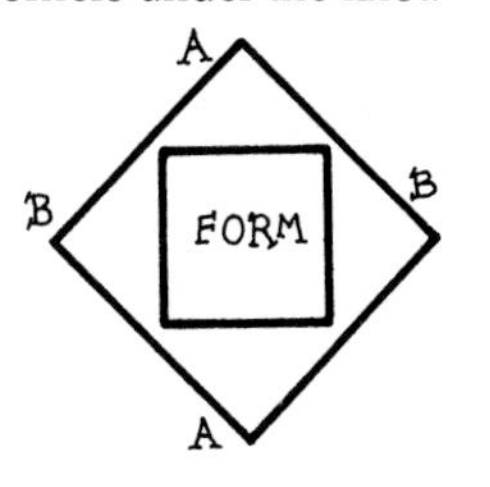

TOYS

ALPHABET BLOCKS (1½″, 3″, 3½″ and 4″ square)

Pictured on pages 27, 37 and 58.

Yardage and Supplies:

Scraps of various soft-colored calicos for blocks and applique, the largest being 4½″ square
Scraps of Wonder-Under™ and Stitch-n-Tear® for machine appliqued letters or hearts
Matching thread
Small amounts of stuffing
Template plastic

To Make Alphabet Blocks:

1. Using plastic, make template for each size block desired.
2. Optional: Machine applique letters or hearts to block sides referring to general machine applique directions in *Glossary of Techniques*. It is easier to machine applique before the squares are cut.
3. Place template on wrong side of fabric, draw around it, and cut out six squares for each block. If machine applique has been done, be sure to center applique on side of block.
4. Sew squares together in numerical sequence following diagram. Stitch using a ¼″ seam allowance, beginning and ending stitching ¼″ from each edge. Leave last seam open.
5. Turn and stuff. Whipstitch opening closed.

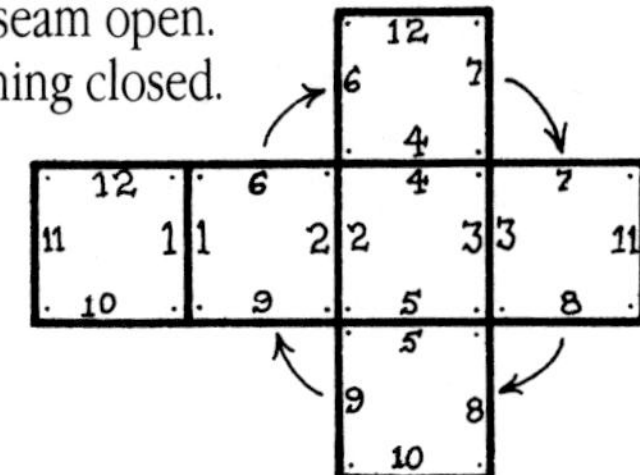

BUNNY RATTLE
Pictured on pages 23 and 37.
Yardage and Supplies:
Fabric (42″-45″)—¼ yd.
Polyester stuffing—small amount
Matching thread
Red pencil
Pink embroidery floss—small amount
Black permanent marking pen
½″ ribbon—¾ yd.
Small plastic egg—approximately 1″ diameter
4-5 small beads

To Make Bunny Rattle:
1. Cut one head back, two head fronts, four bodies. Transfer all markings.
2. With right sides together, and using ¼″ seam allowance, sew center front of head.
3. Stitch head front to head back, matching raw edges; leave open at neck and backstitch at each end of stitching line. Clip and turn right side out. Sew a few stitches across base of each ear. Set aside.
4. Stitch two body sections together at lower center front. Repeat for other set.
5. With right sides together, stitch body sets together along outer edges from neck edge at one side to neck edge at other side, leaving neck open. Stitch inner, center circle from dot to dot, backstitching at each dot. Clip all curves and turn right side out.
6. Stitch upper center front seam from neck edge to dot. Leave upper center back seam open.
7. To make rattle, cut a slit in a plastic egg with the tip of a very sharp knife. Poke a few beads into egg.
8. Put a small amount of stuffing into head. Put in the rattle and pack stuffing tightly around rattle. Stuff body firmly. Whipstitch center opening closed.
9. Pin head to body, tucking in raw edges of neck. Whipstitch in place.
10. Using pink embroidery floss, stitch nose with satin stitch and mouth with stem stitch. Mark eyes with black permanent marking pen. Using the side of the red pencil lead, blush cheeks and inside of ears.
11. Tie ribbon bow around neck.

CLUTCH BALL (3½″ diameter)
Pictured on page 37.
Yardage and Supplies:
Scraps of various soft-colored calicos at least 3″ × 6″
Small amounts of stuffing
Matching thread
Template plastic
Glue gun or tacky glue (optional)

To Make Clutch Ball:
1. Make templates for the semi-circle and the ellipse.
2. Lay *each* template on wrong side of 12 different pieces of fabric and draw around them with a pencil (24 pieces). Cut out on drawn lines.
3. Each segment is composed of a semicircular piece folded down the center and stitched to the ellipse shape. Leave a small opening for turning and stuffing. Use ¼″ seam allowance. Whipstitch or glue opening closed. Make 12 segments.
4. Join all segments at the corners as shown, having the ellipse shape face out.

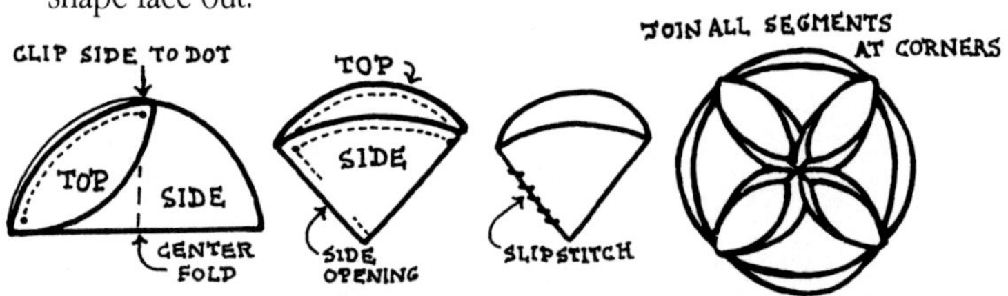

TWENTY-INCH DOLL
Pictured on pages 17, 19, 21, 23, 25, 27, 45 and 58.
Yardage and Supplies:
Fabric (42″-45″):
Body—⅜ yd.
Legs—¼ yd.
Shoes—⅛ yd.
Dress—⅔ yd.
Pantaloons—⅜ yd.
Yarn for hair—1 skein mohair
¼″ elastic—1 yd.
Permanent marking pens—red and black
Powder blush or red pencil
Stuffing—1 lb.
Matching thread
Embroidery floss to match body fabric
Hair ribbons, bows, or trims

Cut:
Body fabric—two bodies and four arms
Leg fabric—four
Shoe fabric—four
Dress fabric—two bodices, two sleeves 8½″ long × 10″ wide, and one skirt 13½″ long × 38″ wide
Pantaloon fabric—two pieces 10″ wide × 12″ long

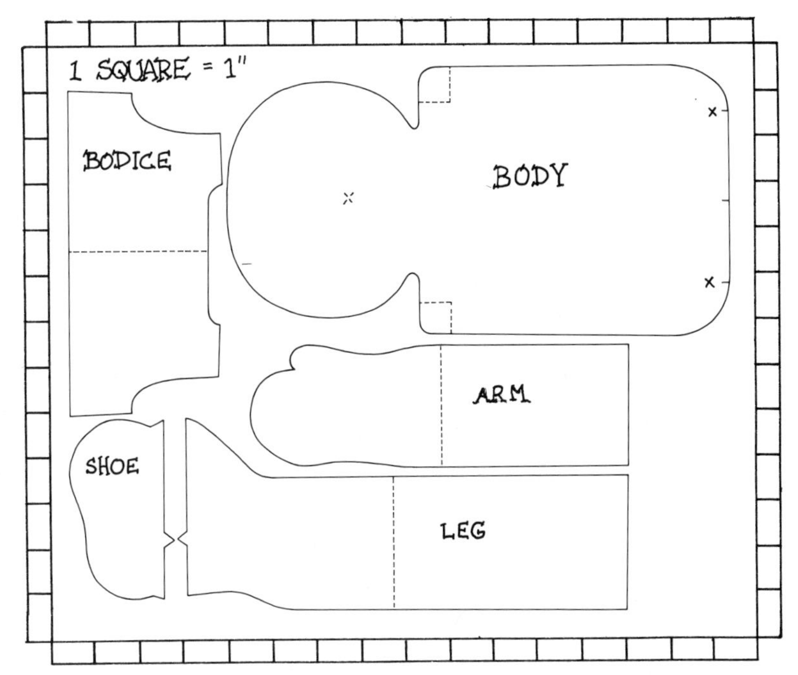

Use ¼″ seam allowance throughout unless otherwise noted.

To Make Body:

1. On **right** side of one body piece, mark placement for eyes, nose and mouth. Mark shoulder seams on right sides of both body pieces. Mark dotted lines on arms and legs.
2. Sew body with right sides together, using ¼″ seam allowance. Leave open between "X's". Clip neck curves. Turn.
3. Matching notches, sew shoes to legs. Sew legs matching stripes. Change thread to match shoes and legs. Leave open at top edges. Clip at ankles. Turn.
4. Sew arms, leaving open at top edges. Clip between fingers and thumbs. Turn.
5. Firmly stuff arms and legs to dotted lines. Cut small pieces of floss and tie tightly around joints at dotted lines.
6. Finish stuffing arms and legs to approximately 1½″ from top. Fold in ¼″ seam allowance on tops of arms.
7. Bring seams together at top of arm and pleat as illustrated.
8. Match marked lines of shoulder seams, front and back, and stitch, forming a triangle.
9. Place arms with thumbs facing front on top of shoulder triangle. Stitch.
10. Pleat legs like arms without turning in ¼″. Center top edges of legs between lines on raw edge of body back, being sure to have legs facing forward. Stitch through back and legs only.

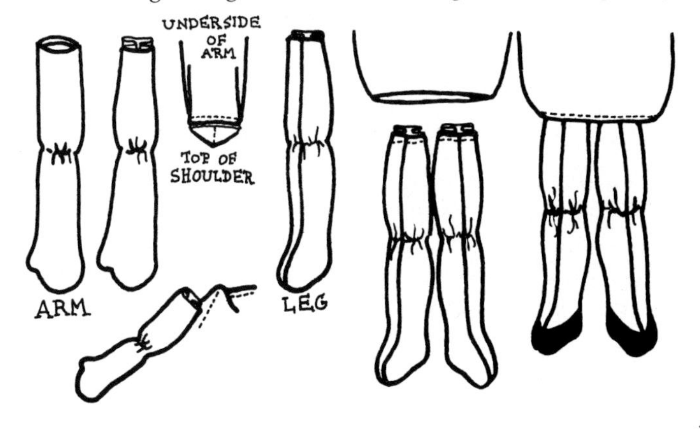

11. Stuff head and body firmly.
12. Turn under ¼″ seam allowance on body front and whipstitch closed.
13. Using permanent marking pens, draw eyes in black and nose and mouth in red. Use the side of the red pencil to blush cheeks, or use powder blush.
14. To make hair, *loosely* wrap yarn approximately 100 times around a 6½″ piece of cardboard, keeping it even and smooth. Draw a 12½″ line on a piece of paper. Without cutting yarn, and working from one end, carefully slide yarn from cardboard and lay it on the piece of paper with loops at one side placed 1″ from marked line and strands of yarn at right angles to marked line. Stitch with matching thread on marked line. Shorter loops will form face curls. Tear paper away. Pin hair to head starting at center back. Lay stitched line on yarn around the crown of head one inch in front of head seam at front center, meeting end of stitched line again at back of head. See illustration. Sew or glue in place. Pull all long hair loops up to top back of head. Make into one ponytail or divide into two. Tie with yarn. Decorate hair as desired using ribbons, bows, or other trims.

To Make Dress:

1. Using dotted line on pattern, slit one bodice section down the center to form two bodice backs.
2. With right sides together, sew shoulder seams of front and back bodices.
3. Narrowly hem (approximately ⅛″) back edges of bodice and neckline.

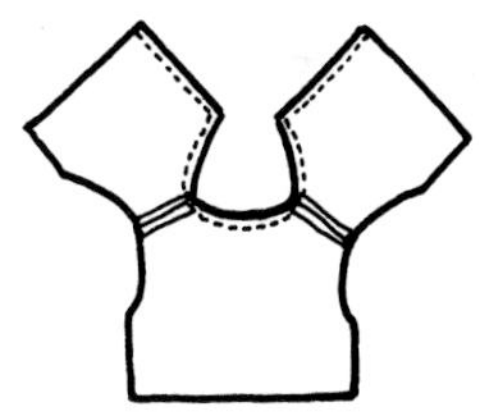

4. Run two rows of gathering threads (⅛″ apart and ¼″ from edge) along one 10″ edge of each sleeve.
5. Mark center of sleeve and match to shoulder seam. Pull up gathers to fit armhole. Stitch.
6. Narrowly hem lower edge of each sleeve. Draw a line on the wrong side of each sleeve from side to side ¾″ above bottom edge. Straight stitch or zig-zag stitch ¼″ elastic over line, pulling tight while stitching to gather.
7. With right sides together, sew sleeve seam and bodice side seam in one continuous motion. Repeat for other side.
8. On one 38″ edge of skirt, run two rows of gathering ⅛″ apart and ¼″ from edge.
9. Mark this edge of skirt into four equal sections.
10. Sew the two short edges of skirt right sides together.
11. Press up a 2½″ hem along bottom edge of skirt. Topstitch hem in place, folding in raw edge while stitching.
12. Gather top edge of skirt to fit bodice, matching seam of skirt to center back of bodice. Stitch.
13. Dress doll and tack dress closed at neckline.

To Make Pantaloons:

1. On wrong side of fabric, mark inner leg seam following diagram. With right sides together, sew ¼″ away from both sides of marked inner leg seam.

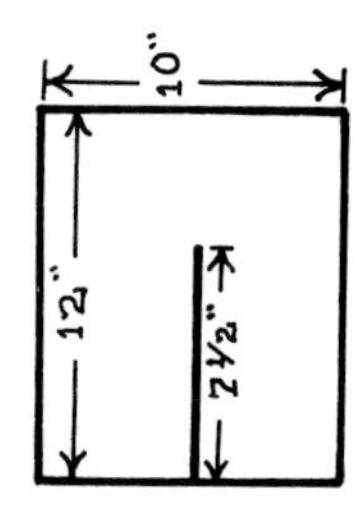

2. Cut marked line to stitching.
3. Narrowly hem lower edge of each leg. Draw a line on the wrong side of each leg from side to side 1″ above bottom edge. Straight stitch or zig-zag stitch ¼″ elastic over line, pulling tight while stitching to gather.
4. With right sides together, sew outer leg seams.
5. Turn right side out and press.
6. Press ¼″ to wrong side on waist edge. Press over ⅜″ again and stitch near fold, leaving 1″ unstitched to insert elastic. Insert a 10″ piece of elastic through casing. Secure ends and complete stitching for casing.

For ordering full-size doll pattern, see end of *ACCESSORIES* section.

PENTAGON BABY BALL (4″ diameter)

Pictured on page 37.

Yardage and Supplies:

Scraps of soft-colored calicos at least 3½″ square
Small amount of stuffing
Matching thread
Template plastic

To Make Pentagon Ball:

1. Make a template of pentagon pattern.
2. Lay template on wrong side of 12 different pieces of fabric and draw around it with a pencil. Cut out on drawn lines.
3. Stitch using a ¼″ seam allowance. Sew pentagons together in numerical order following illustration. Begin and end stitching ¼″ from each edge.
4. Make two halves, then match peaks to valleys to join halves. Turn and stuff firmly. Fold under raw edges and whipstitch opening closed.

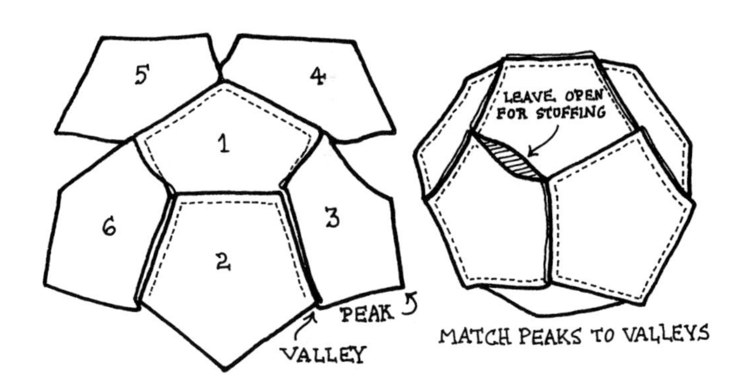

WALLHANGINGS

HANDPRINT WALLHANGING (9″ × 36″)

Pictured on pages 43 and 61.

Yardage and Supplies:

Pink check—¼ yd.
Light print (includes backing)—½ yd.
Pink fabric (includes binding)—½ yd.
Matching thread
Batting—1 piece at least 11″ × 38″
Brown or tan fabric paint

To Make Wallhanging:

1. Cut of pink check:
   Five 5½″ squares
   Cut of light print:
   10 pieces 1″ × 5½″ (A)
   10 pieces 1″ × 6½″ (B)
   1 piece 11″ × 38″ for backing
   Cut of pink:
   4 pieces 1¼″ × 6½″ (C)
   2 pieces 1¾″ × 33½″ (D)
   2 pieces 1¾″ × 9″ (E)
   3 pieces 2½″ × fabric width for binding
2. Assemble: Stitch "A" to sides of each block; stitch "B" to top and bottom of each block.
3. Join blocks together with "C".
4. Stitch "D" to each side.
5. Stitch "E" to top and bottom.
6. Cut one piece of batting 11″ × 38″.
7. Layer backing, batting, and wallhanging top. Baste.
8. Hand or machine quilt in the ditch around outer edge of each frame. Trim edges even with top.
9. Finish edges by sewing binding to sides first and then to top and bottom.
10. To make handprints—pour a small amount of fabric paint into a tin pie plate. With a brush or your fingers, spread paint evenly but sparingly over bottom of pie plate. Lay child's hand flat on paint and then lay flat on fabric square being careful to center handprint. Too much paint will give a muddy appearance. To make the wallhanging a "growth chart", add a handprint once a year.

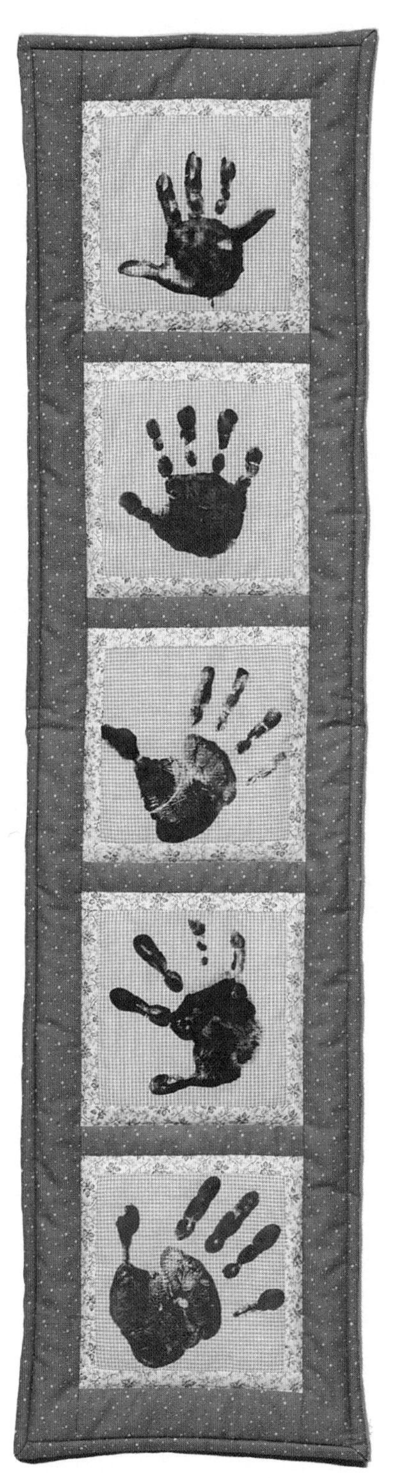

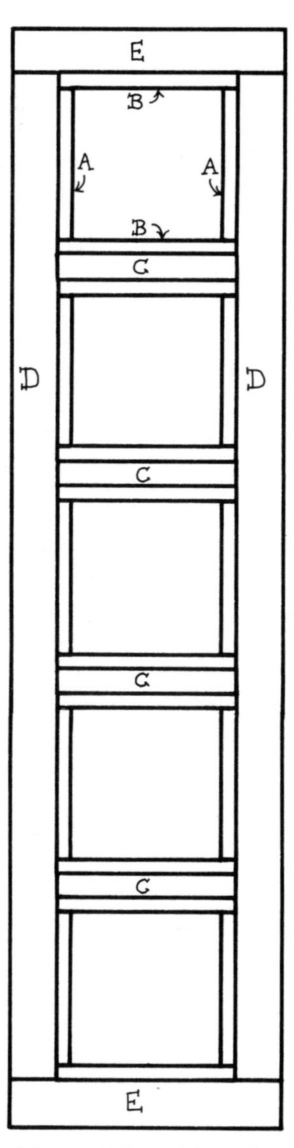

HANDPRINT AND HOMESPUN HEART WALLHANGING

HOMESPUN HEART WALLHANGING (9″ × 36″)
Pictured on page 45.

Yardage and Supplies:

Light tan (blocks, backing)—⅝ yd.
Black check (includes binding)—½ yd.
Red—1/6 yd. (¼ yd. of a lengthwise stripe)
Hearts—scraps at least 5″ square
Matching thread
Batting—1 piece at least 11″ × 38″

To Make Wallhanging:

1. Cut of light tan:
   - Five 5½″ squares
   - 1 piece 11″ × 38″ for backing

   Cut of black check:
   - 4 pieces 1¼″ × 6½″ (C)
   - 2 pieces 1¾″ × 33½″ (D)
   - 2 pieces 1¾″ × 9″ (E)
   - 3 pieces 2½″ × fabric width for binding

   Cut of red:
   - 10 pieces 1″ × 5½″ (A)
   - 10 pieces 1″ × 6½″ (B)

   Cut of scraps:
   - 5 hearts using template I
2. Hand or machine applique hearts to center of each tan square.
3. Assemble: Stitch "A" to sides of each block; stitch "B" to top and bottom of each block.
4. Join blocks together with "C".
5. Stitch "D" to each side.
6. Stitch "E" to top and bottom.
7. Cut one piece of batting 11″ × 38″.
8. Layer backing, batting, and wallhanging top. Baste.
9. Hand or machine quilt around each heart and each frame. Trim edges even with top.
10. Finish edges by sewing binding to sides first and then to top and bottom.

PINWHEELS WALLHANGING (12″ × 31″)

Pictured over end of crib on page 37.

Yardage and Supplies:

Print (blocks, frames, binding)—⅝ yd.
Pink, green, and lavender—⅛ yd. each or scraps 9″ × 9″
Muslin (includes backing)—1 yd.
Matching thread
Batting—1 piece at least 14″ × 33″

To Make Wallhanging:

1. Cut and piece three blocks following cutting and sewing directions for *Pinwheels* quilt, page 36.
2. Cut of print:
   6 pieces 1″ × 7½″ for side block frame (A)
   6 pieces 1″ × 8½″ for top and bottom block frame (B)
   3 pieces 3″ × fabric width for binding
   Cut of muslin:
   2 pieces 2″ × 8½″ (C)
   2 pieces 2¼″ × 27½″ (D)
   2 pieces 2¼″ × 12″ (E)
   1 piece 14″ × 33″ for backing
3. Assemble: Stitch "A" to sides of each block; stitch "B" to top and bottom of each block.
4. Join top and bottom blocks to middle block with "C".
5. Stitch "D" to each side and "E" to top and bottom.
6. Cut 1 piece of batting 14″ × 33″.
7. Layer backing, batting, and wallhanging top. Baste.
8. Hand or machine quilt in the ditch around each print frame and each pinwheeel. Trim edges even with top.
9. Finish edges by sewing binding to sides first and then to top and bottom using a ½″ seam allowance.
10. To make three tabs for hanging, cut three pieces of print fabric 2½″ × 4″. Fold in half lengthwise and stitch the long edges. Turn right side out. Fold each in half with seam centered on inside. Tuck in raw edges and whipstitch one to each upper corner and one to center of top edge of wallhanging.

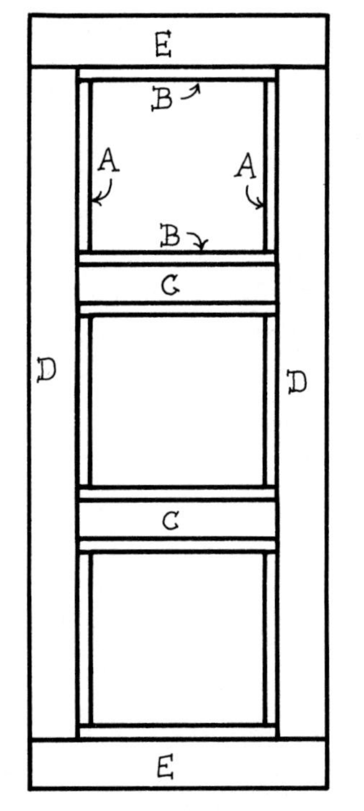

PINWHEELS WALLHANGING

The doll shown throughout the book is a variation of DreamSpinner pattern #128, *Molly's Toys. Molly's Toys* features a full-size pattern for a 20″ body. Also included are dress, pinafore, pantaloons, cat and blocks. To order this full-size pattern, send $4.50 plus $1.50 for postage and handling.

The large bear found on pages 17 and 33 and in the photograph on the back of the book is *Bittersweet Bear,* DreamSpinner pattern #114. Directions are included for a quilt to sew and cut up to make the bear. To order this full-size pattern, send $4.50 plus $1.50 for postage and handling.

Send to:
DreamSpinners
Dept. PS
8970 E. Hampden Avenue
Denver, Colorado 80231
Or Call: (303) 740-6206

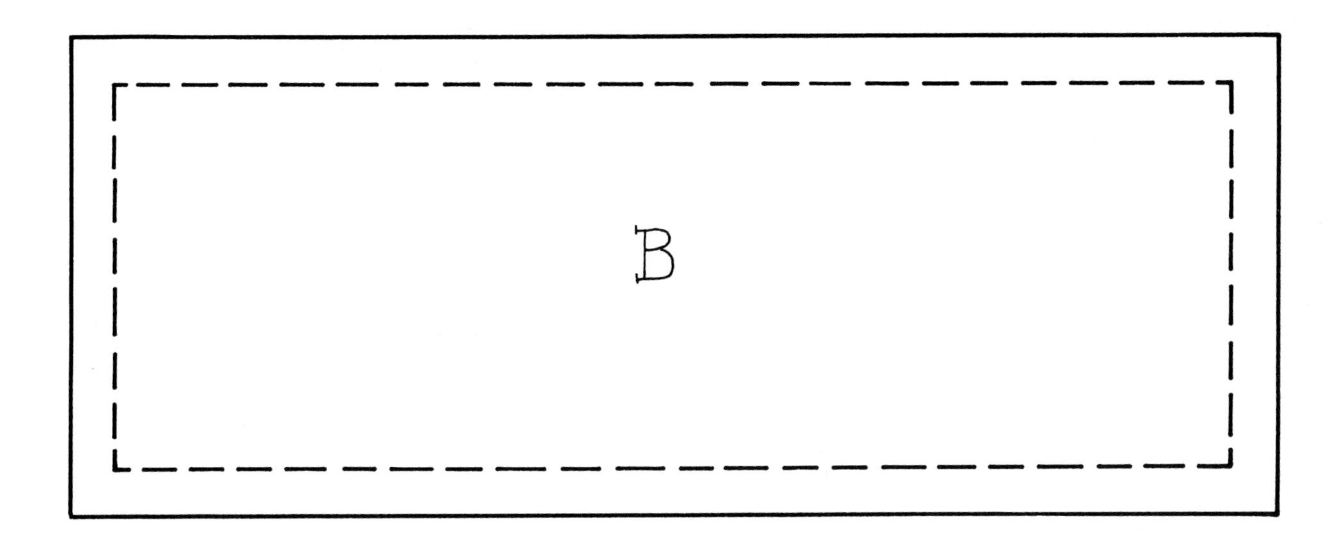
B

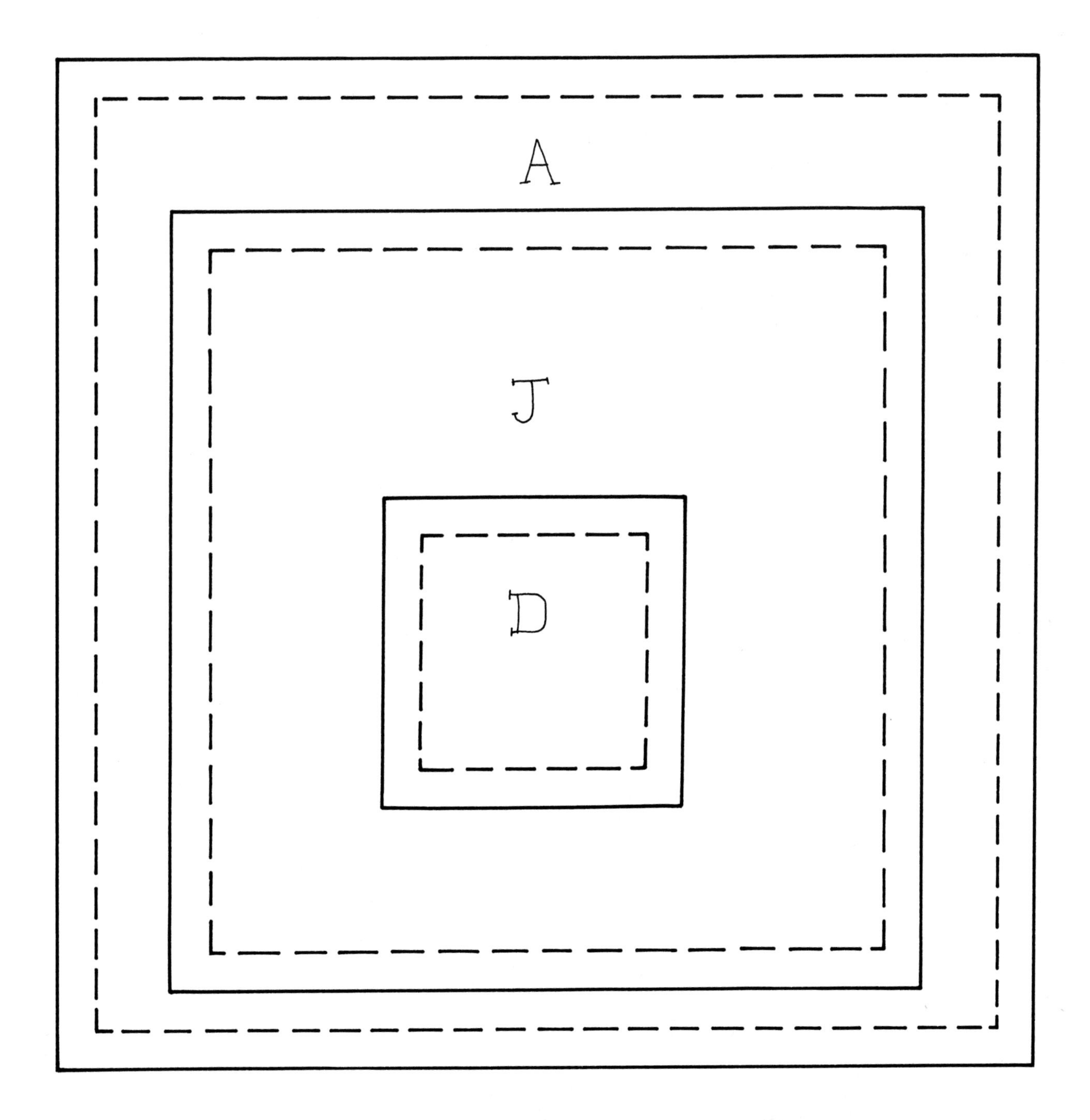
A
J
D

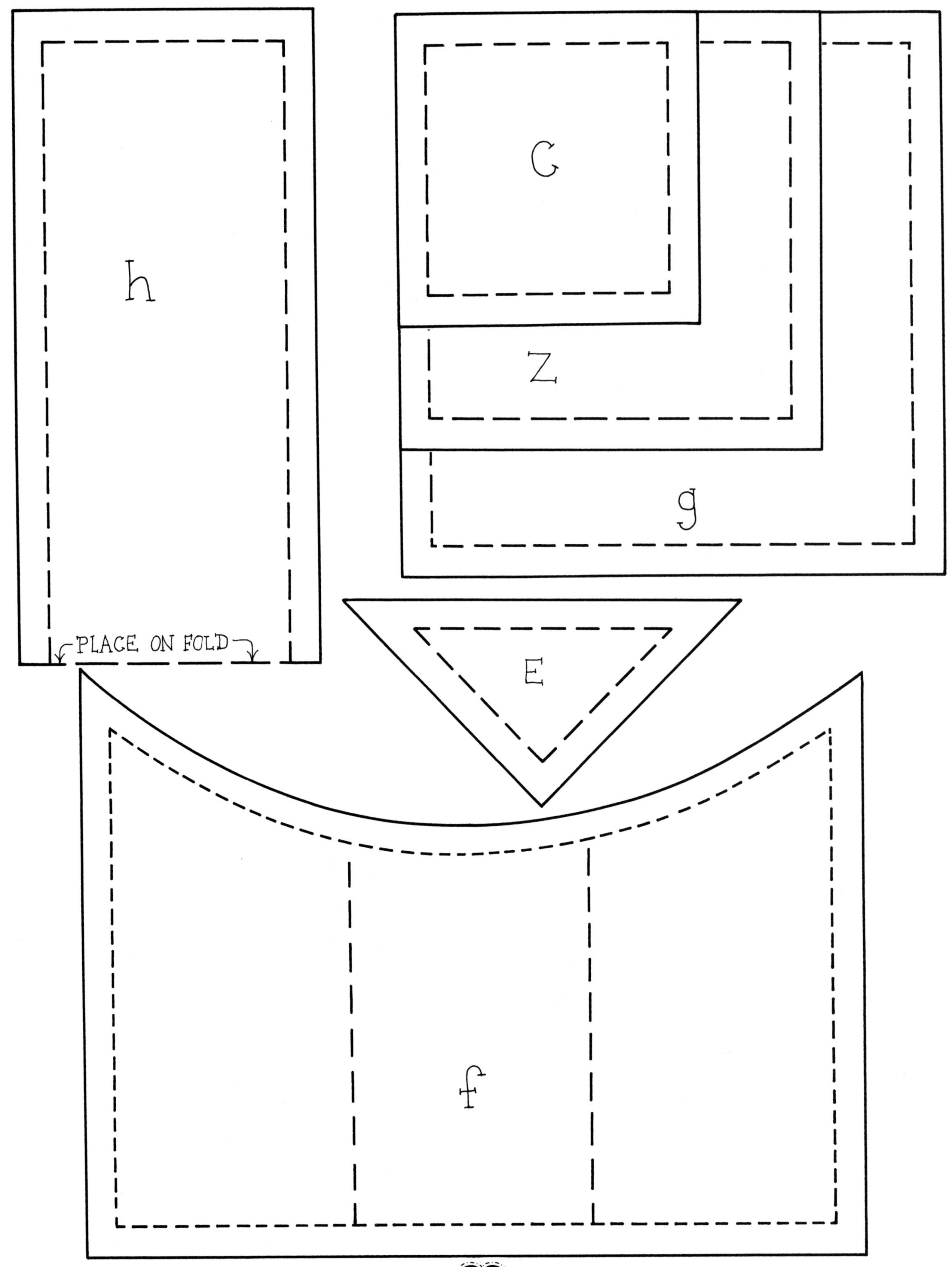
h
PLACE ON FOLD
C
Z
g
E
f

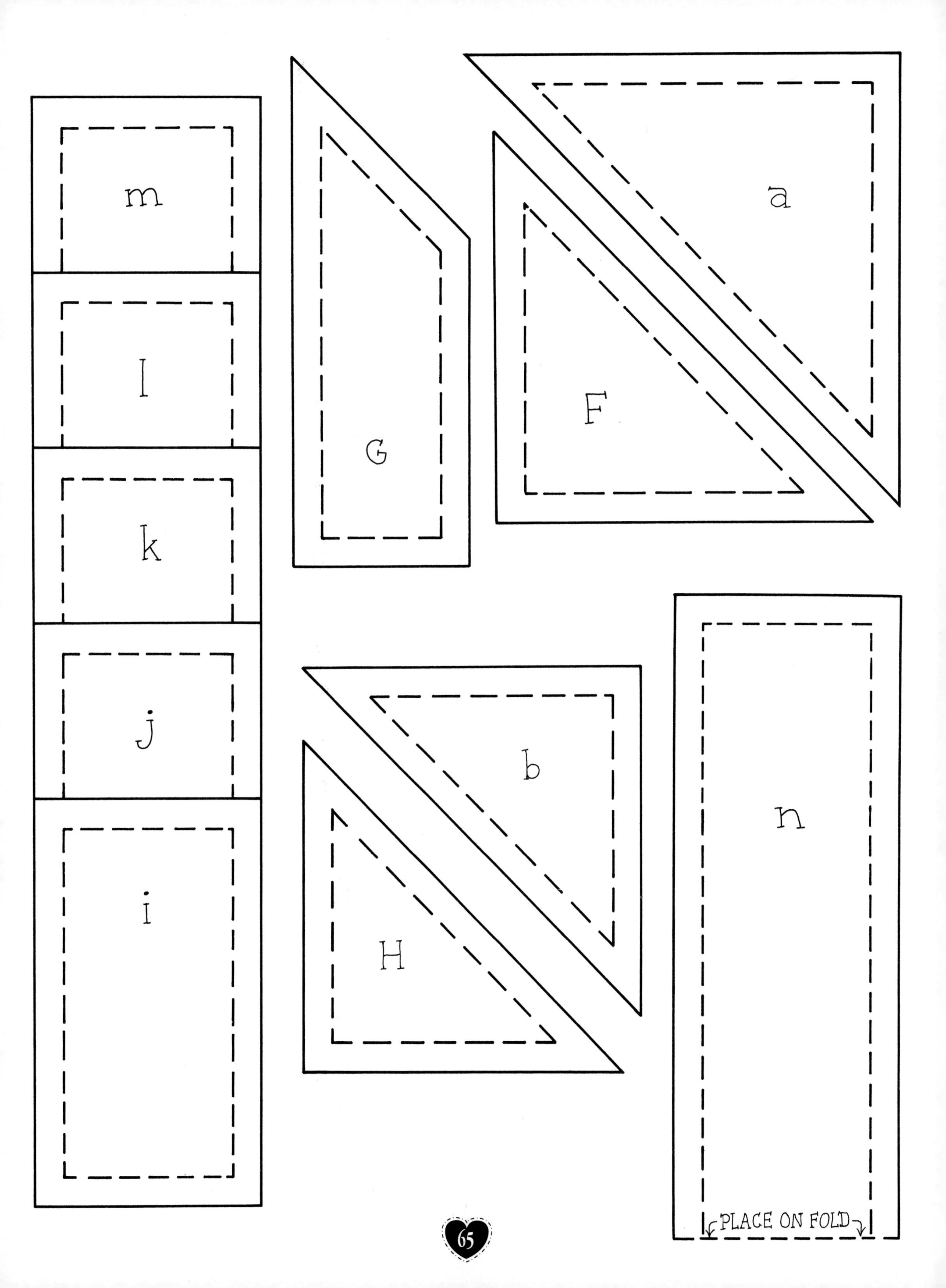
m
l
k
j
i
G
a
F
b
H
n
PLACE ON FOLD

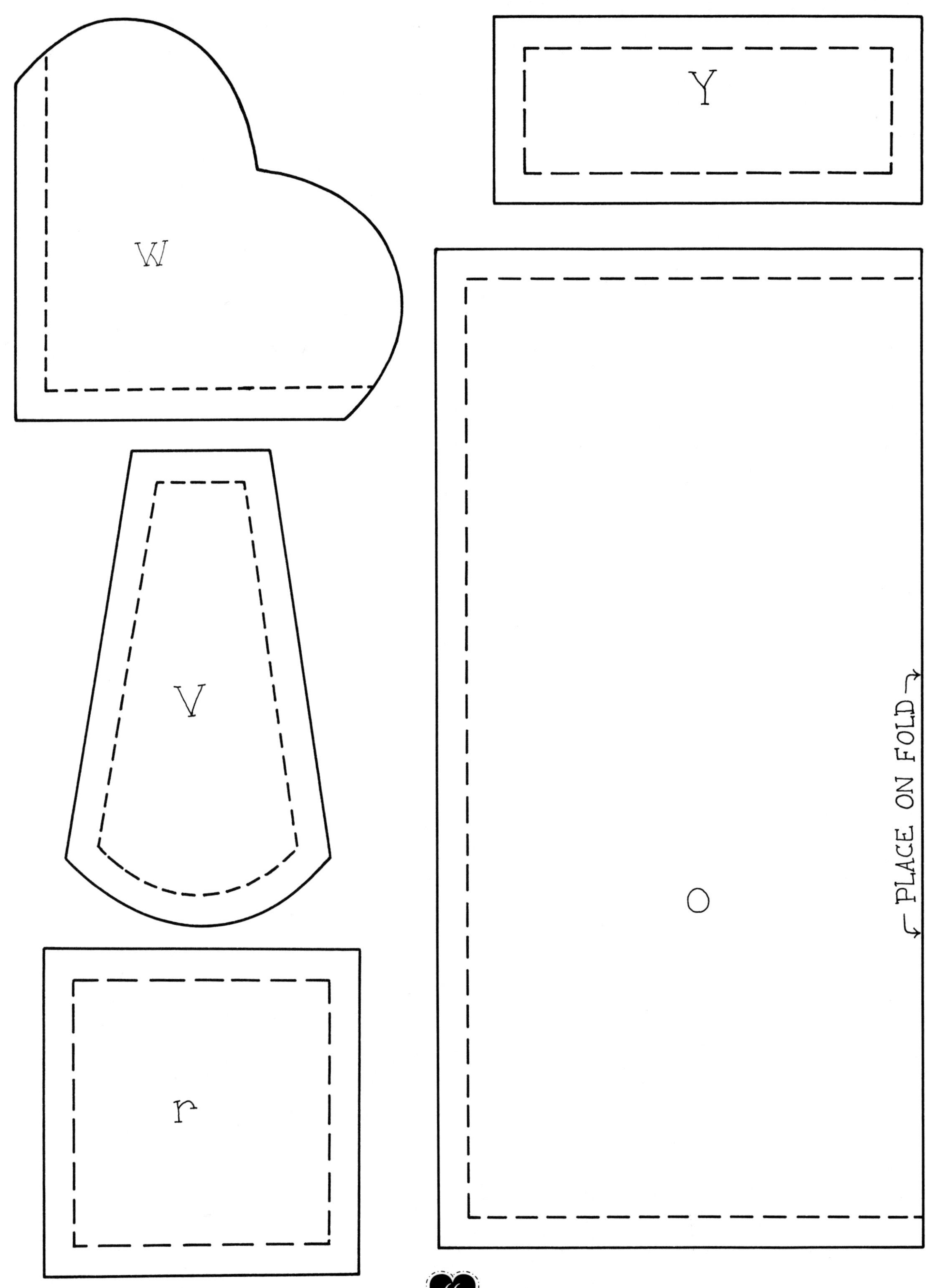
Y
W
V
PLACE ON FOLD
O
r

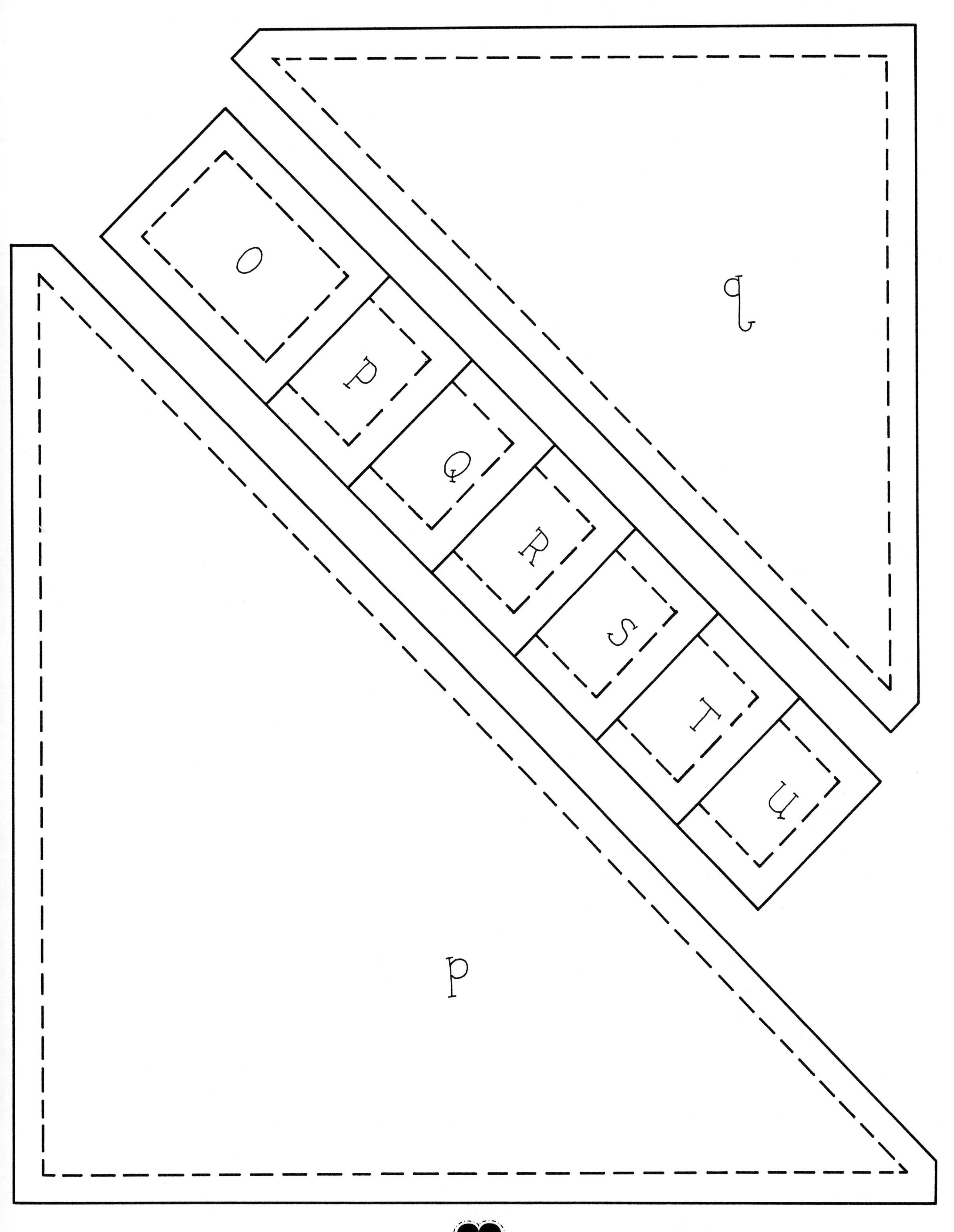
O
P
Q
R
S
T
U
q
p

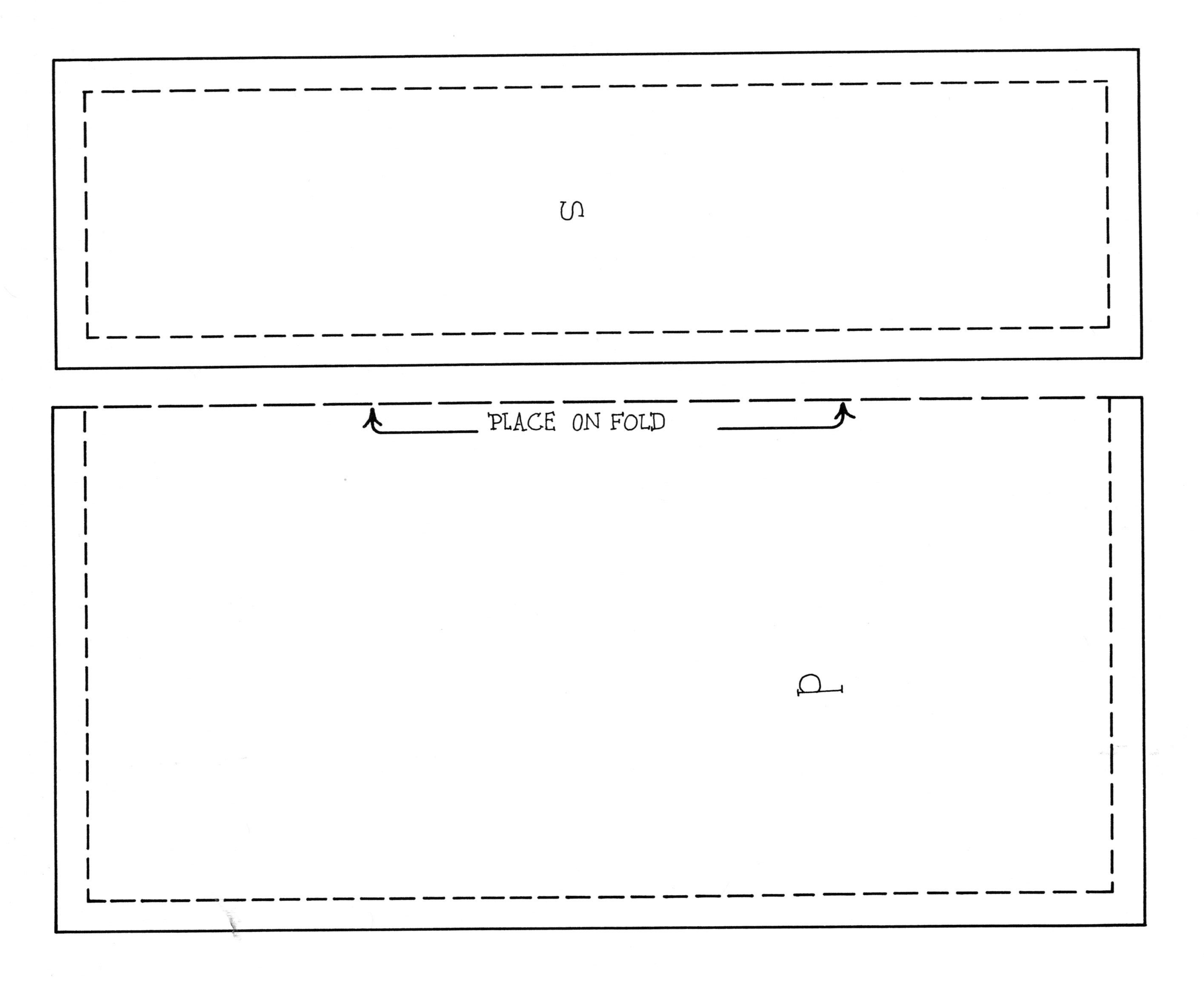
S
PLACE ON FOLD
P

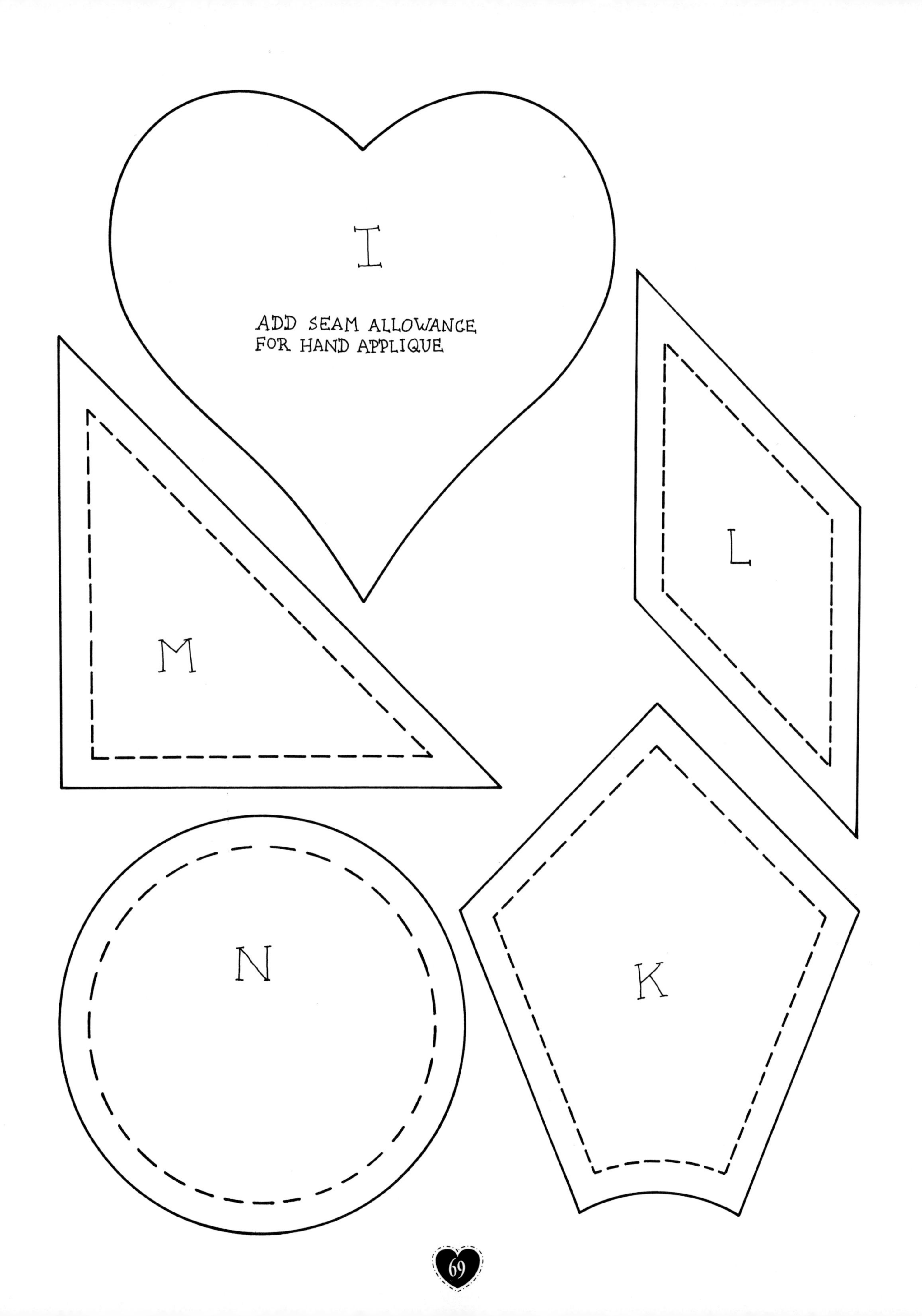
I
ADD SEAM ALLOWANCE
FOR HAND APPLIQUE
L
M
N
K

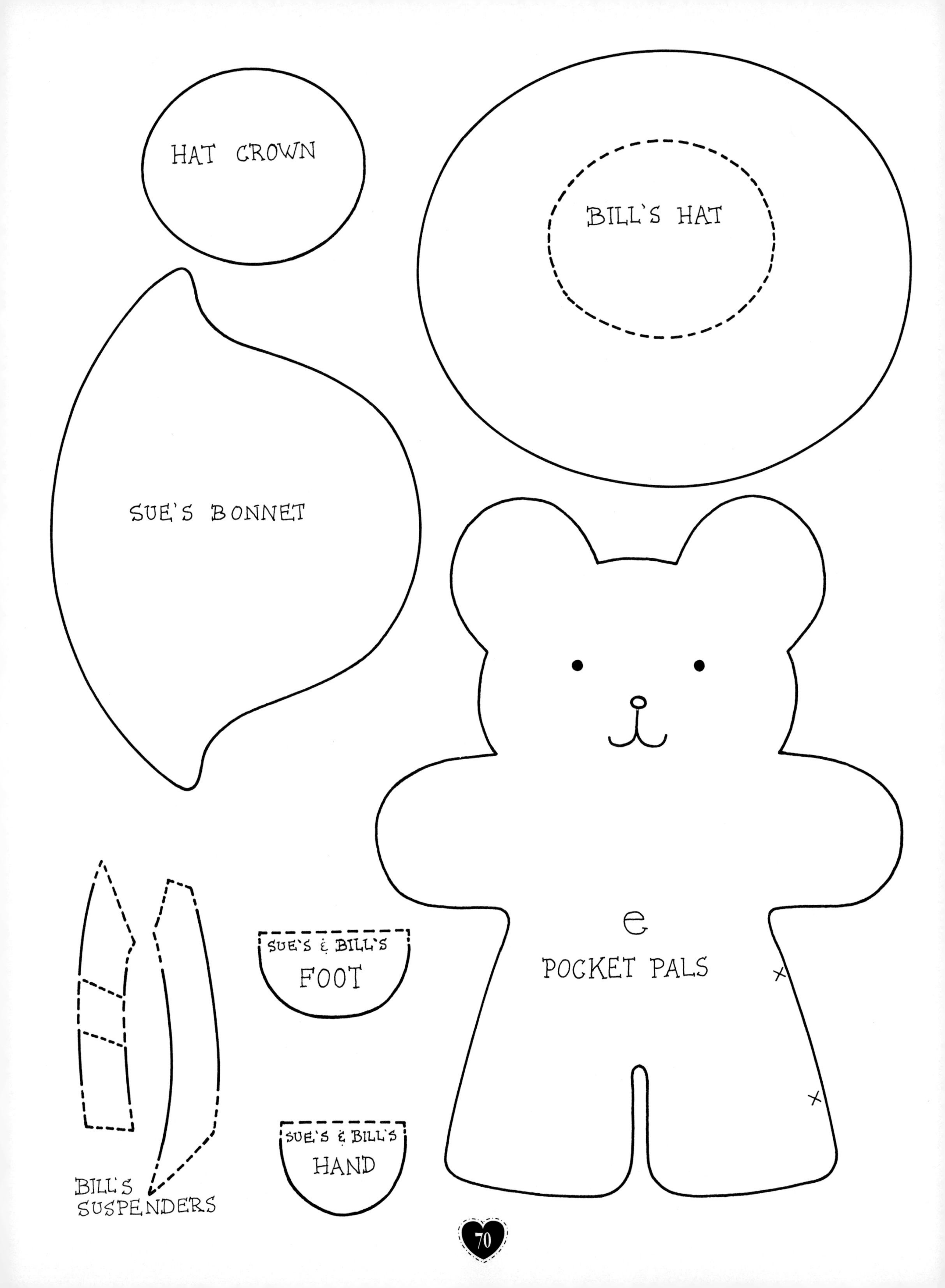
HAT CROWN
BILL'S HAT
SUE'S BONNET
e
POCKET PALS
SUE'S & BILL'S
FOOT
SUE'S & BILL'S
HAND
BILL'S
SUSPENDERS

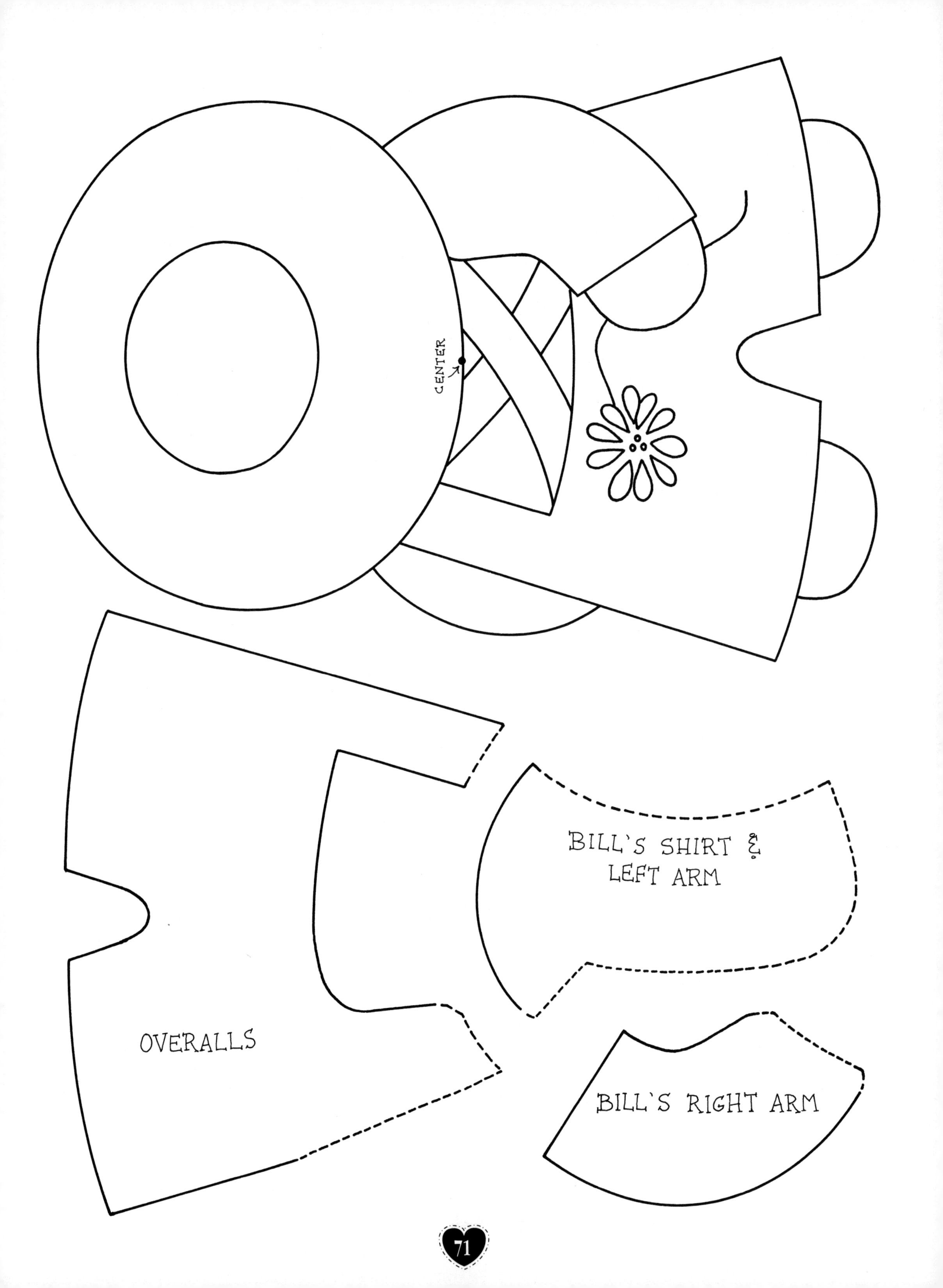
CENTER
BILL'S SHIRT &
LEFT ARM
OVERALLS
BILL'S RIGHT ARM

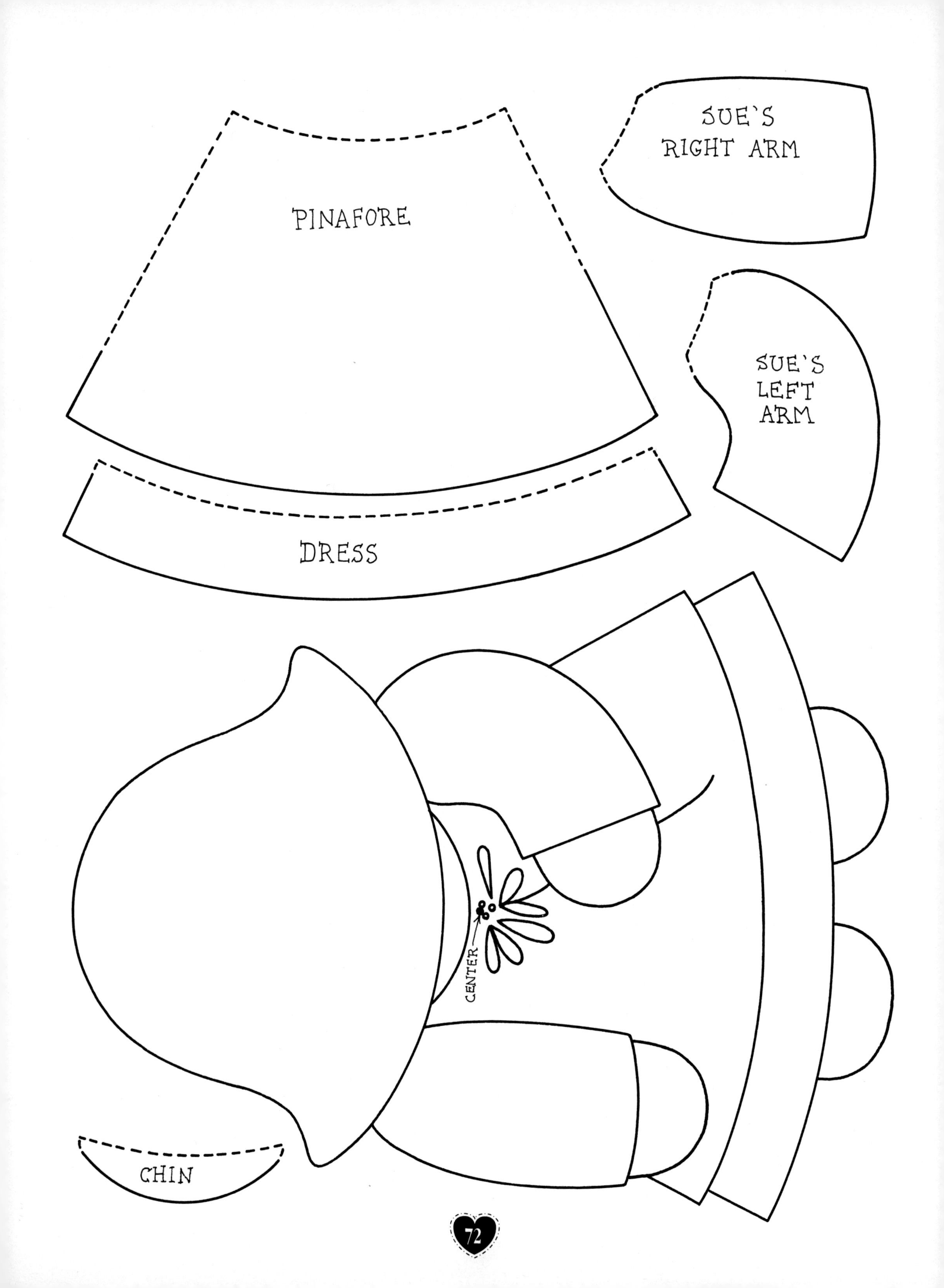
PINAFORE
SUE'S RIGHT ARM
SUE'S LEFT ARM
DRESS
CENTER
CHIN

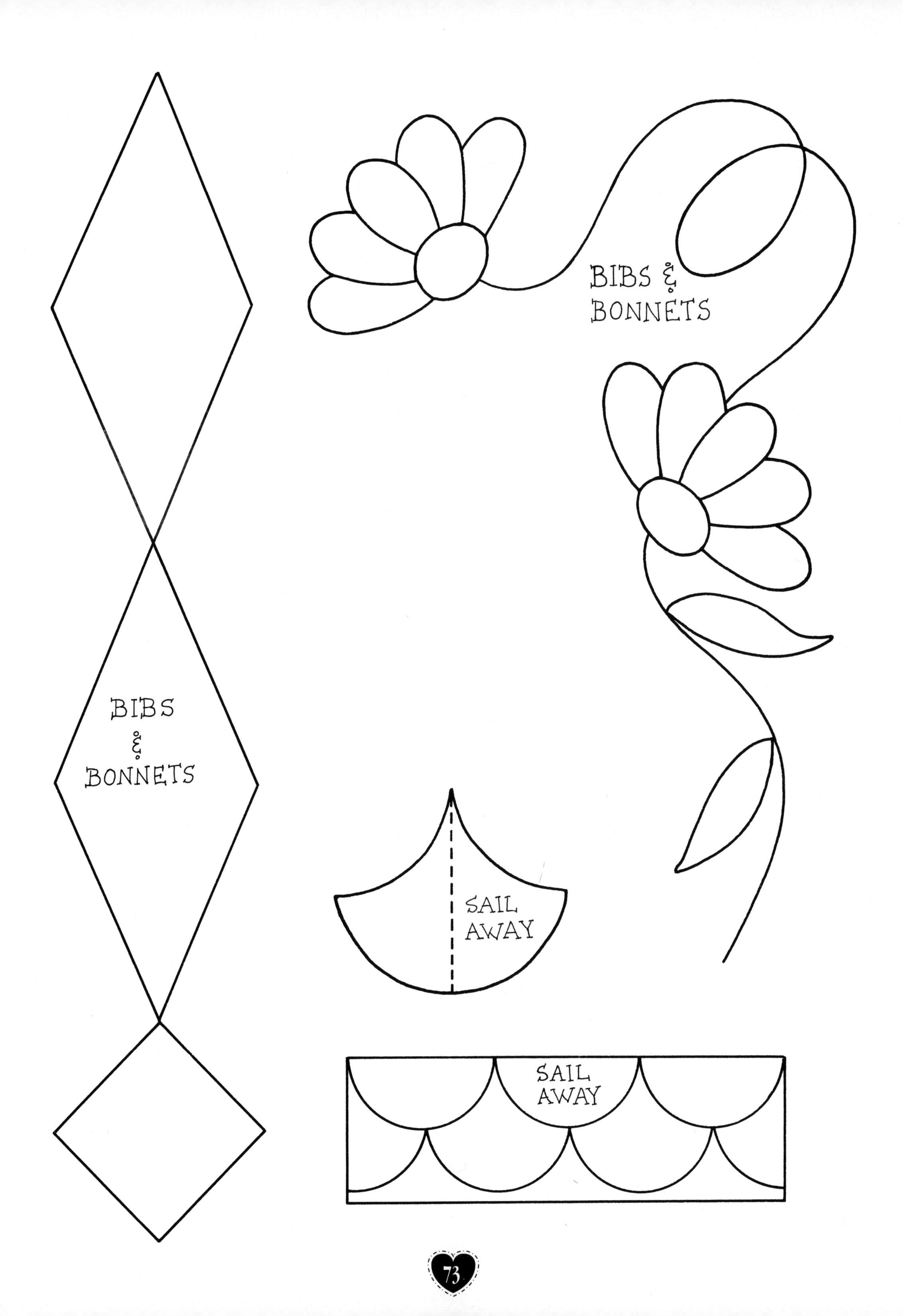
BIBS &
BONNETS
BIBS
&
BONNETS
SAIL
AWAY
SAIL
AWAY

HEART OF MY HEART
POCKET
PALS

GARDEN SONG
BABY TEARS
MOBILE HEART
MOBILE

DAISY
DAISY
CLUTCH
BALL
HANGING
HEARTS
PENTAGON
BALL
CLUTCH
BALL

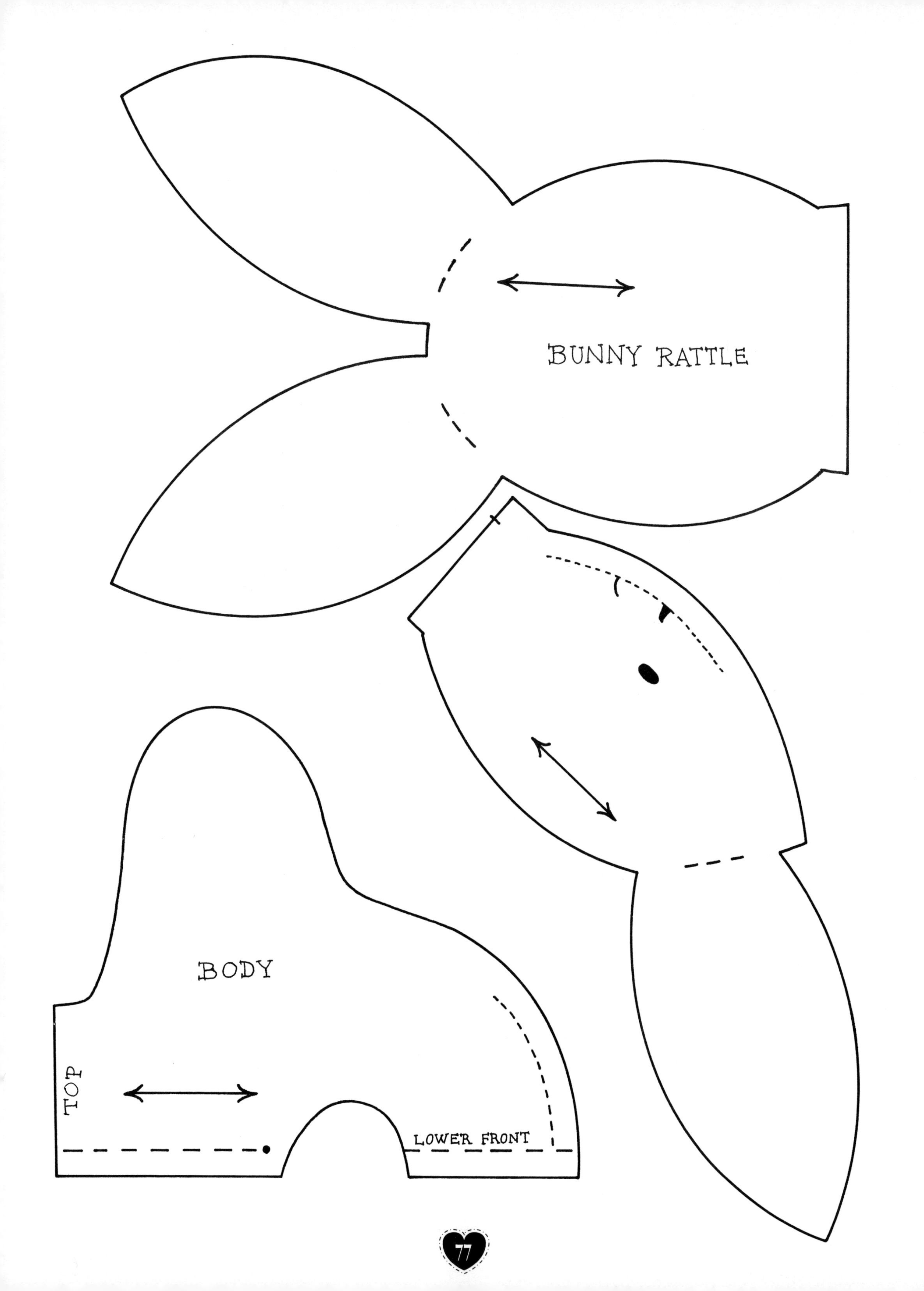
BUNNY RATTLE
BODY
TOP
LOWER FRONT

PSI
YOU
ALPHABET BLOCKS
1½"
3"
3½"
4"

PS
I
YOU

P.S. I LOVE YOU

M. ROBINSON

THE SUN CAME UP THIS MORNING
ITS PROMISE SWEET AND LONG.
A NEW CHILD SHARES THIS DAY WITH ME.
THE BIRDS BEGIN THEIR SONG.

A SPECIAL GIFT OF SQUARES AND STRIPS
WAS SEWN FOR BABY'S COVER.
THE SPARKLING PATCHES QUITE REFLECT
OUR FEELINGS FOR EACH OTHER.

THE BEAUTY OF THE DAYS AHEAD
ARE SEWN IN EVERY SEAM.
I'LL WRAP YOU UP AND HOLD YOU TIGHT
AND ANTICIPATE THE DREAM.